Anita R. Smale

WORKING PAPERS

Chapters 1–11

ACCOUNTING

Canadian Sixth Edition

Charles T. Horngren
Stanford University

Walter T. Harrison, Jr.
Baylor University

Linda Smith Bamber
University of Georgia

W. Morley Lemon
University of Waterloo

Peter R. Norwood
Langara College

Toronto

0-13-123363-7

Executive Editor: Samantha Scully
Developmental Editor: Anita Smale, CA
Production Editor: Mary Ann McCutcheon
Production Coordinator: Deborah Starks

2 3 4 5 09 08 07 06 05

Printed and bound in Canada

Contents

To the Student

These Working Papers are a set of handy tear-out forms for your convenience in solving all exercise and problem assignments from Chapters 1–11 of *Accounting* by Horngren, Harrison, Bamber, Lemon, and Norwood.

These forms will save you time. You can solve problems neatly and systematically on forms that fit the specific problem requirements.

Arrangement of Forms

The forms are numbered in the same way as the textbook exercises and problems, and are arranged in the same order. Long forms, such as work sheets, appear as foldout pages in the back of the book. When you reach a problem that requires a foldout, you will find an instruction directing you to the correct form.

Comments about the Working Papers are encouraged.

Please send any comments to me in care of Pearson Education Canada at **phcinfo.pubcanada@pearsoned.com**.

Anita R. Smale, C.A.

NAME
SECTION
DATE

Chapter 1

E1-1

E1-2

NAME
SECTION
DATE

E1-3

a. – e.

E1-4

a. – j.

NAME
SECTION
DATE

E1-5

	Assets	=	Liabilities	+	Owner's Equity
Business A	________		$123,600		$168,800
Business B	$ 91,800		________		$ 68,000
Business C	$163,400		$119,600		________

COMPUTATIONS:

E1-6

O/E = A − L

4000 + 24000 − 2000 − 14000 = 28000 − 16000 = 12000

E1-7

Requirements 1 & 2

A=L+O/E

NAME
SECTION
DATE

E1-8

a. – i.

a. Increase asset (Cash)
Increase owner's equity (Owner, Capital)

b. decrease asset (Cash) (-2000)
decrease O/E (expense) (-2000)

c. decrease asset (cash) (-2700)
increase asset (supplies) (+2700)

d. Increase asset (Account receivable) (5000)
Increase O/E (Revenue) (5000)

e. Increase A (office equ) (5000)
Increase L (Account payable) (5000)

(f) Increase A (cash) 3000
~~Increase O/E~~ Decrease A (Account Receivable) 3000

g. Decrease A (cash) -1000
~~Increase A~~ (account payable) +1000
Decrease L

h.

NAME
SECTION
DATE

E1-9

Analysis of Transactions

DATE	ASSETS		= LIABILITIES + OWNER'S EQUITY			
						TYPE OF OWNER'S EQUITY TRANSACTION

NAME
SECTION
DATE

E1-10

Requirements 1 a. – h.

Requirement 2

NAME
SECTION
DATE

E1-11

Requirement 1

Requirement 2

Requirement 3

NAME
SECTION
DATE

E1-12

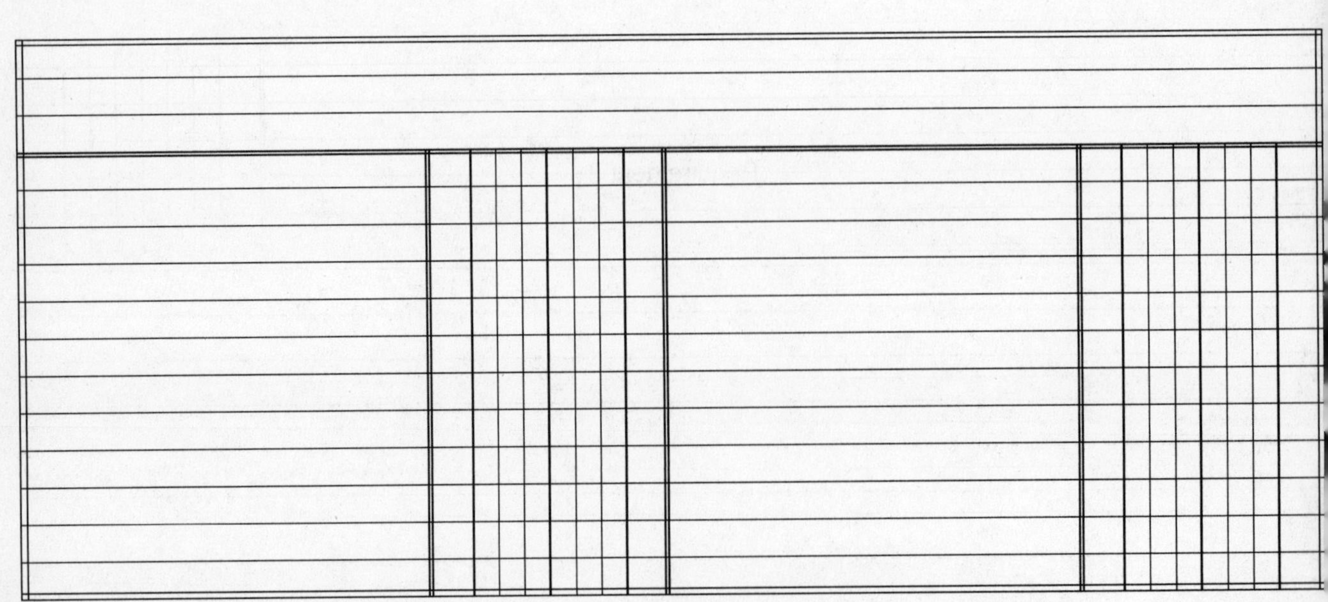

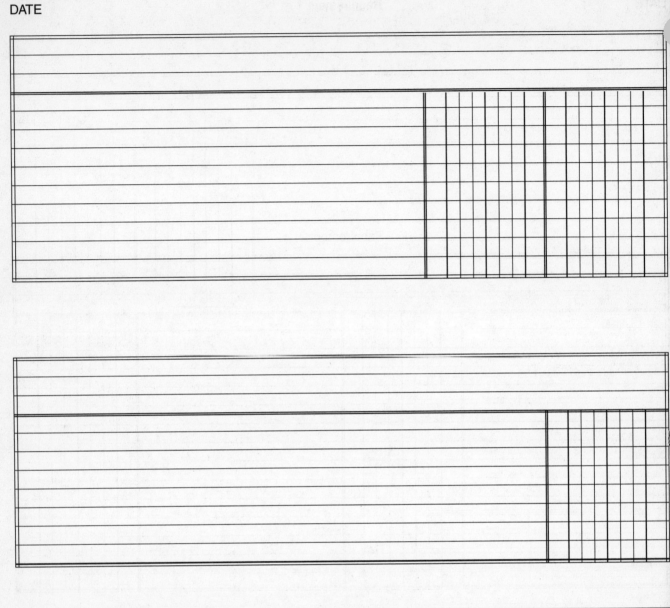

NAME
SECTION
DATE

E1-13

Requirement 1

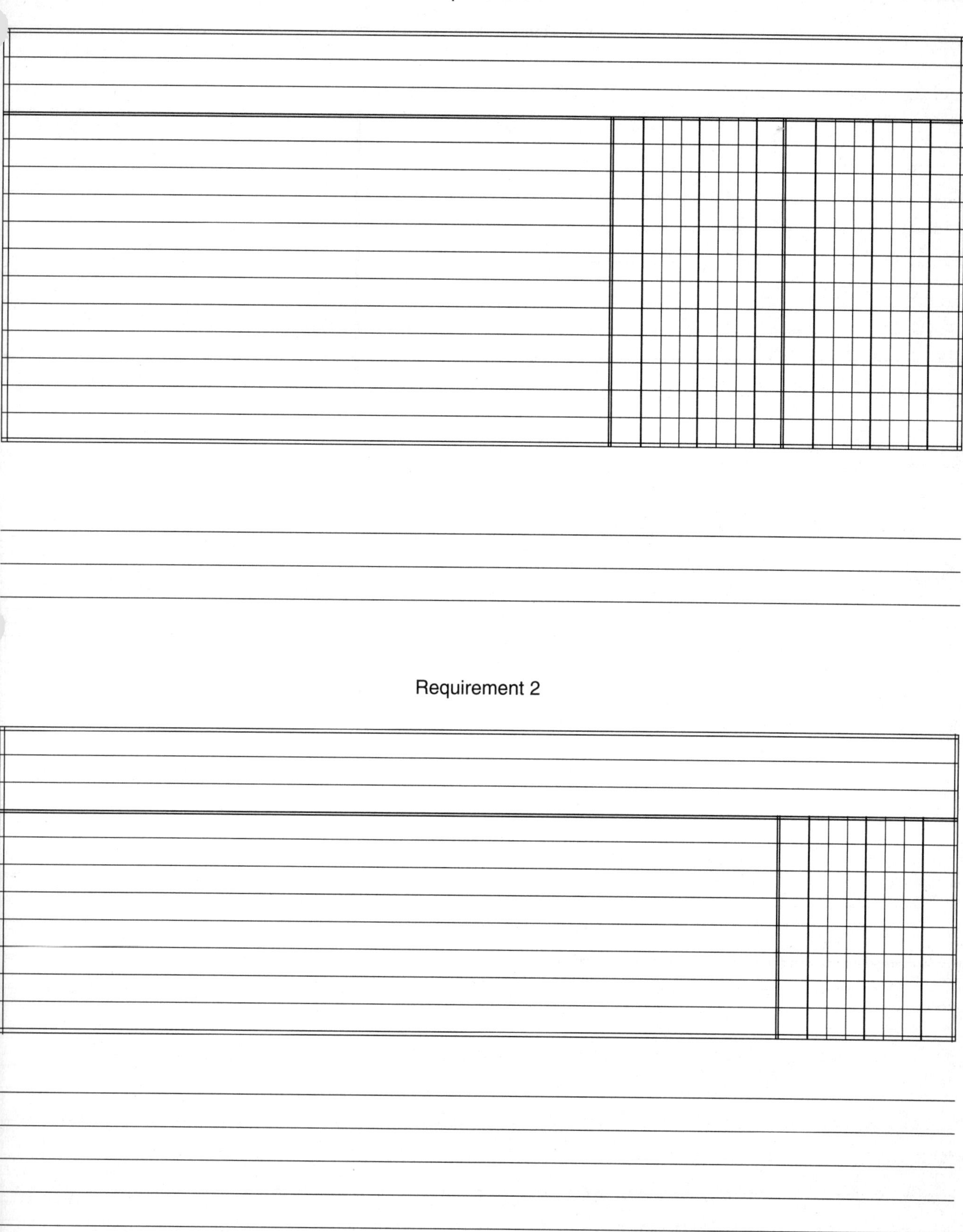

Requirement 2

NAME
SECTION
DATE

E1-14

Requirement 1 – 3

NAME
SECTION
DATE

E1-15

ACCOUNT	OAK CO.	CEDAR CO.	MAPLE CO.

Computations:

NAME
SECTION
DATE

Beyond the Numbers 1–1

Beyond the Numbers 1–2

a. – c.

INCOME STATEMENT

BALANCE SHEET

NAME
SECTION
DATE

Ethical Issue 1

Requirements 1–3

Ethical Issue 2

Requirements 1 & 2

P1-1A

Requirement 1

CLASSIFICATION OF TRANSACTIONS

July 1		July 6	
2		7	
3		9	
5		23	
5		31	

NAME
SECTION
DATE

PAGE 35

P1-1A
(Continued)

Requirement 2

Analysis of Transactions

DATE	ASSETS				= LIABILITIES + OWNER'S EQUITY		
	CASH	Accounts Recievable	Supplies	Office Furniture	Accounts payable	owners equity	TYPE OF OWNER'S EQUITY TRANSACTION
July 1st	NO ENTRY, NOT A BUSINESS TRANSACTION						
July 2nd	NO ENTRY, NOT A BUSINESS TRANSACTION						
July 3rd	NO ENTRY, NOT A BUSINESS TRANSACTION						
July 5th	+ 200,000					+ Capital 200,000	Sarah's deposit.
July 5th	- 3,800					- 3,800	Rent expense
July 6th	NO ENTRY, NOT A BUSINESS TRANSACTION						
July 7th	- 1,100		+ 1,100				Letterhead stationary.
July 9th			+ 19,000		+ 19,000		Office Furniture
July 23rd		+ 6,000				+ 6,000	Services
July 31st	- 2,000					- 2,000	Personal Expenses.
					19,000	200,200	
TOTAL		$ 219,200			= 219,200		
Aug 23rd	+ 6,000	- 6,000					
	225,200						

NAME
SECTION
DATE

P1-2A

Requirement 1

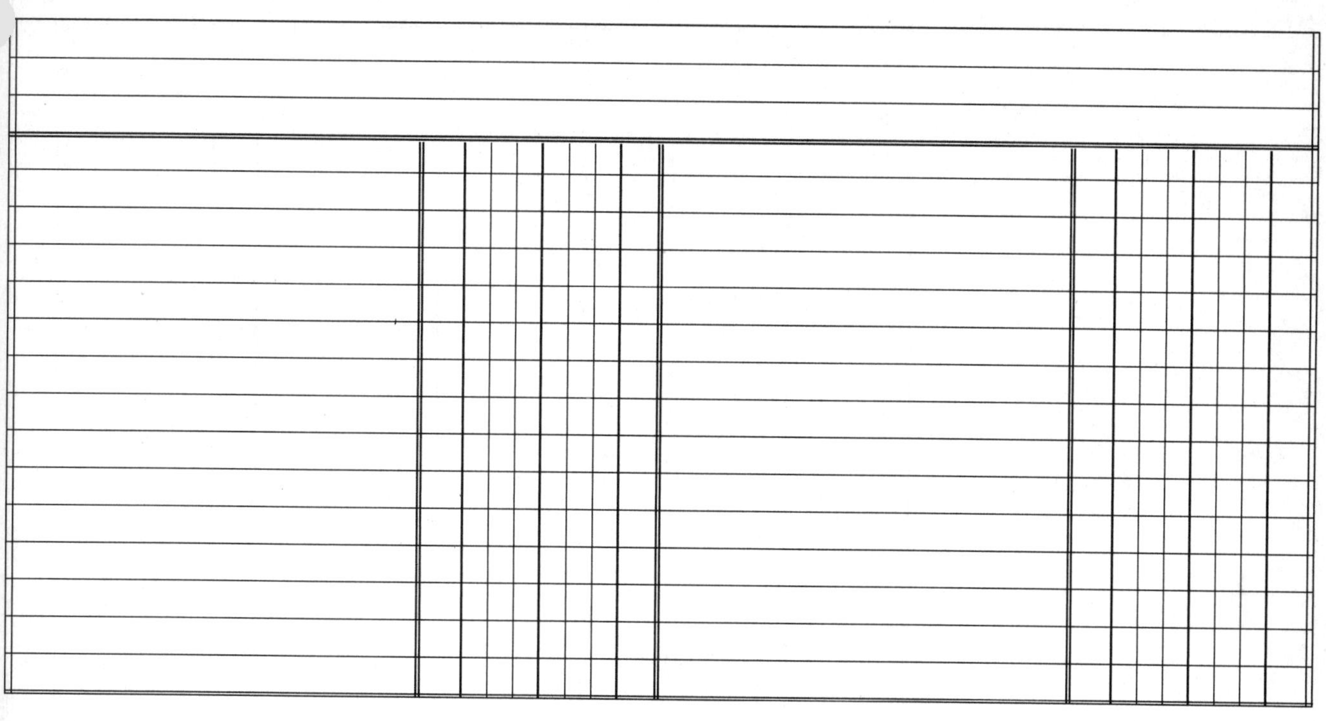

Requirement 2

NAME
SECTION
DATE

P1-3A

Requirement 1

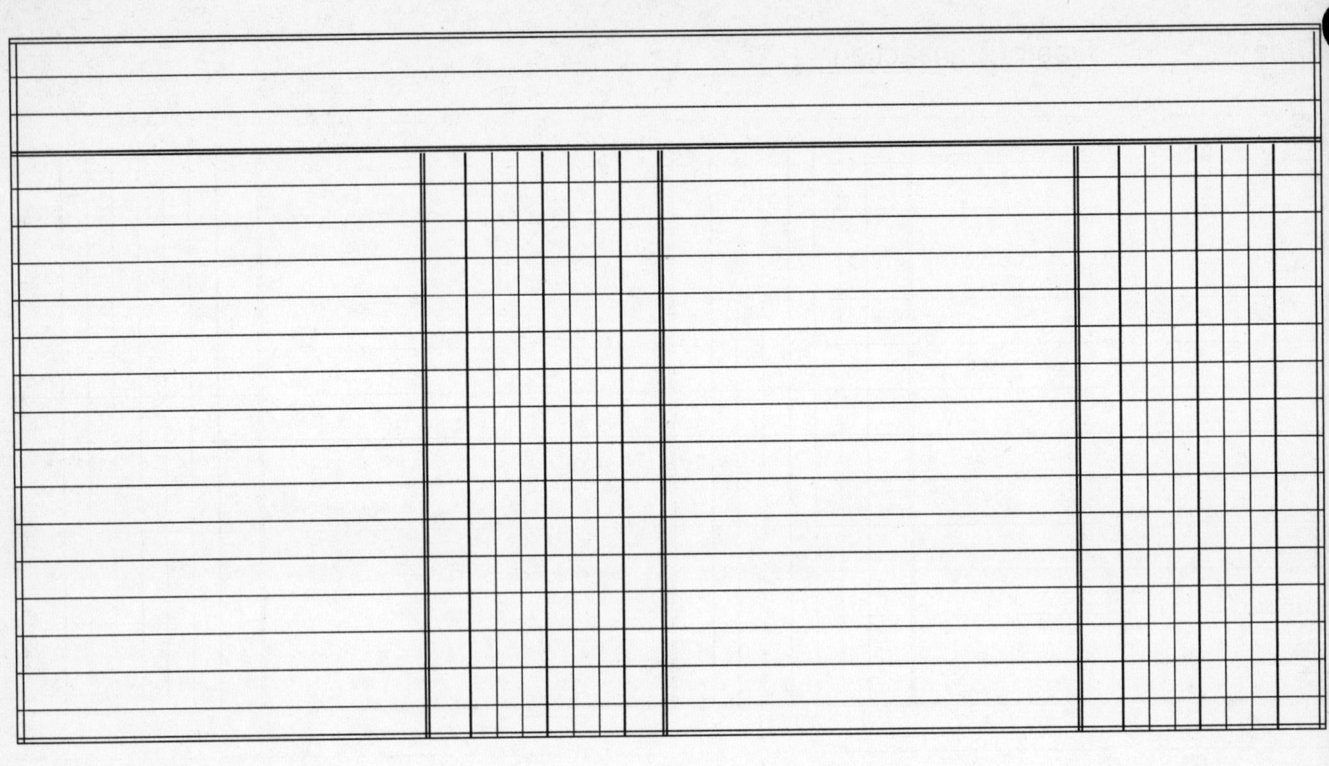

Requirement 2

NAME
SECTION
DATE

P1-4A

Date	Type of Transaction

NAME
SECTION
DATE

P1-5A

Requirement 1

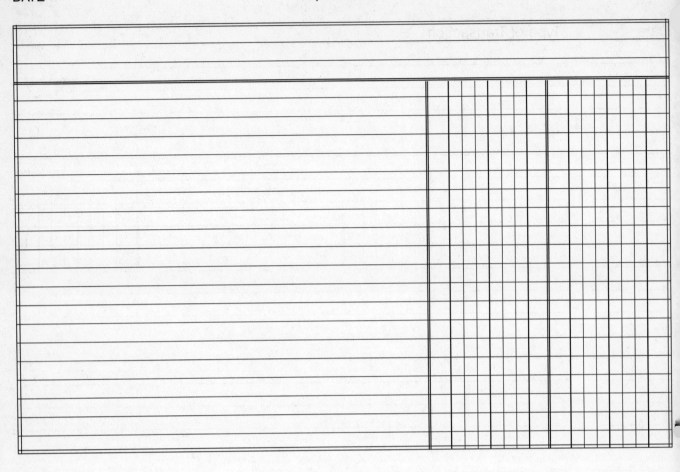

Requirement 2

NAME
SECTION
DATE

P1-5A
(Continued)

Requirement 3

Requirements 4 a. – c.

NAME
SECTION
DATE

P1-6A

Requirement 1

Analysis of Transactions

DATE	ASSETS			= LIABILITIES + OWNER'S EQUITY			TYPE OF OWNER'S EQUITY TRANSACTION

NAME
SECTION
DATE

P1-6A
(Continued)

Requirement 2

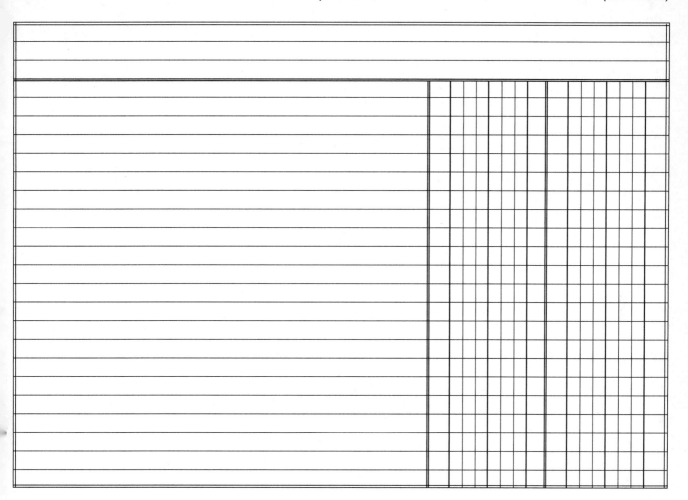

Requirement 3

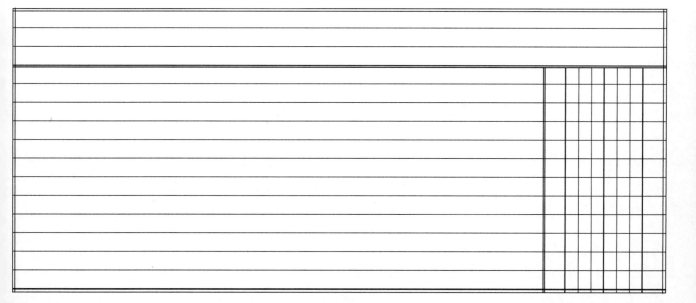

NAME
SECTION
DATE

P1-6A
(Continued)

Requirement 4

NAME
SECTION
DATE

P1-7A

June 1

June 3

June 10

June 18

June 22

June 28

NAME
SECTION
DATE

P1-8A

Requirement 1

NAME
SECTION
DATE

P1-8A
(Continued)

Requirement 2

Analysis of Transactions

DATE			ASSETS			= LIABILITIES + OWNER'S EQUITY		TYPE OF OWNER'S EQUITY TRANSACTION

NAME
SECTION
DATE

Requirement 3

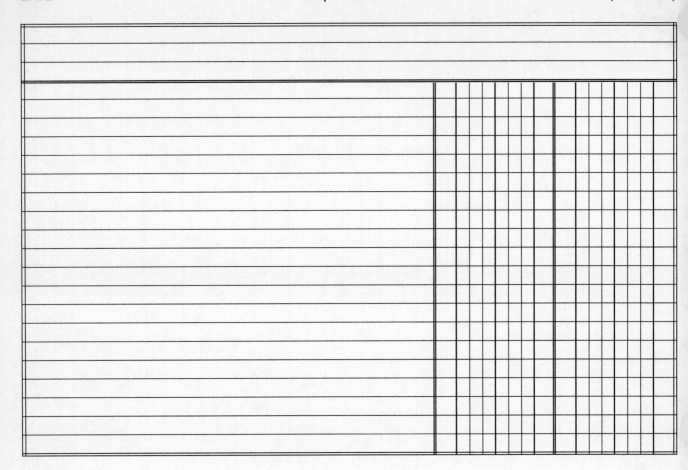

Requirement 4

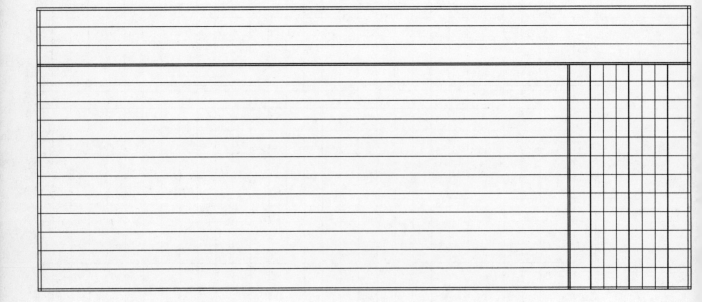

NAME
SECTION
DATE

P1-8A
(Continued)

Requirement 5

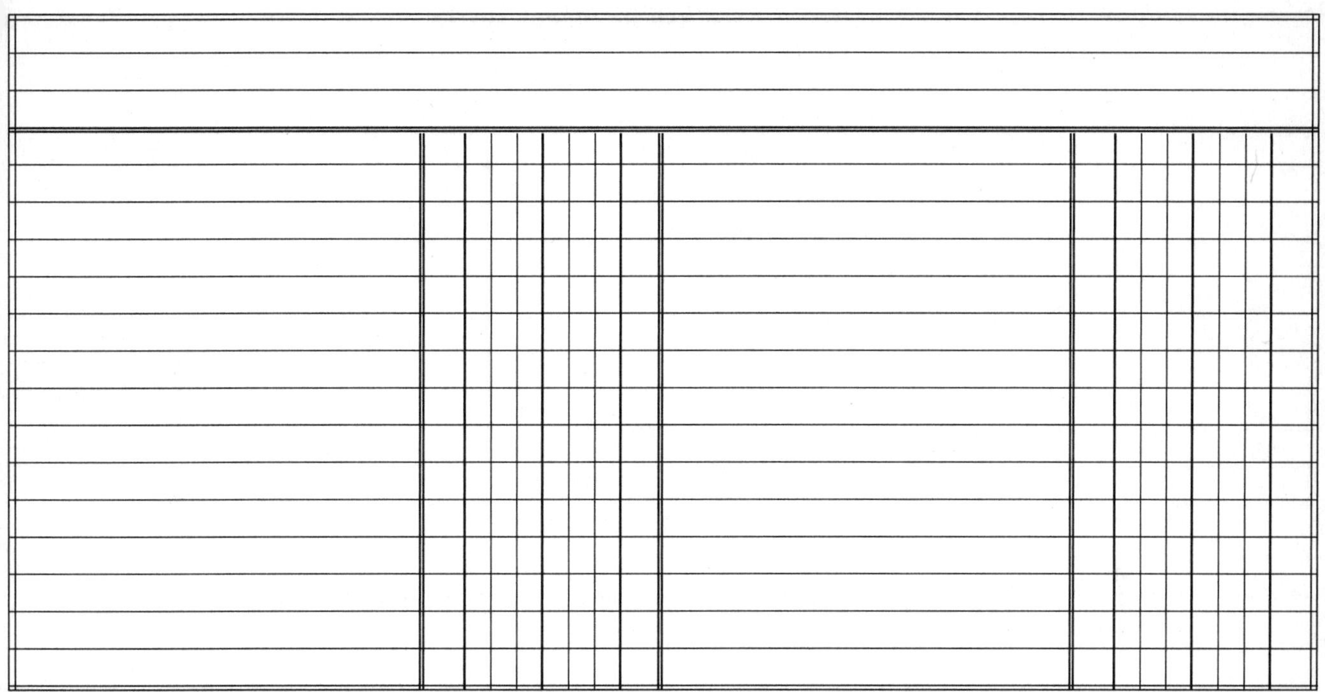

Requirement 6

NAME
SECTION
DATE

P1-1B

Requirement 1

CLASSIFICATION OF TRANSACTIONS

July 4	______________	July 10	______________
5	______________	11	______________
5	______________	12	______________
6	______________	29	______________
7	______________	31	______________

P1-2B

Requirement 1

Requirement 2

NAME Farzana
SECTION PAGE 40
DATE SEPTEMBER 20/04

Requirement 2

P1-1B
(Continued)

Analysis of Transactions

DATE	ASSETS				= LIABILITIES + OWNER'S EQUITY		
	CASH	Accounts Recievable	Supplies	Office Furniture	Accounts Payable	Owner's Equity	TYPE OF OWNER'S EQUITY TRANSACTION
July 4th	NOT A	BUSINESS	TRANSACTION				
July 5th	+105,000					+105,000	investment money
July 5th	- 1,800					- 1,800	
July 6th	-450		+450				Office letterhead
July 7th				+12,000	+12,000		Office Furniture
July 10th	NOT A	BUSINESS	TRANSACTION.				
July 11th	NOT A	BUSINESS	TRANSACTION.				
July 12th	Not A	BUSINESS	TRANSACTION.				
July 29th		+7,500				+ 7,500	Bill for services
July 31st	- 1,500					- 1,500	withdrawl
					12,000	109,200	
TOTAL:	=	121,200		=	121,200		

NAME
SECTION
DATE

P1-3B

Requirement 1

Requirement 2

NAME
SECTION
DATE

P1-4B

Date	Type of Transaction

NAME
SECTION
DATE

P1-5B

Requirement 1

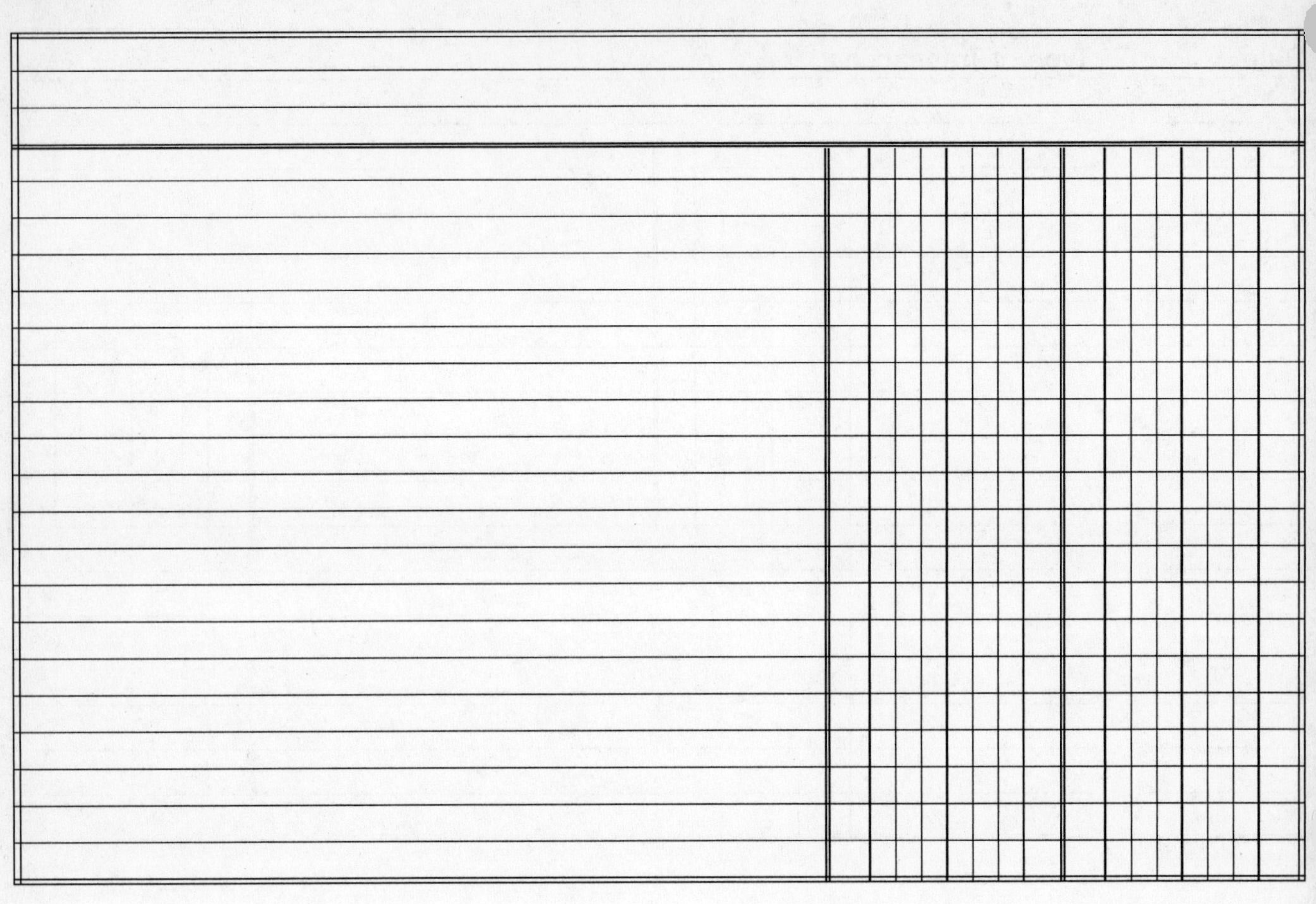

Requirement 2

NAME
SECTION
DATE

P1-5B
(Continued)

Requirement 3

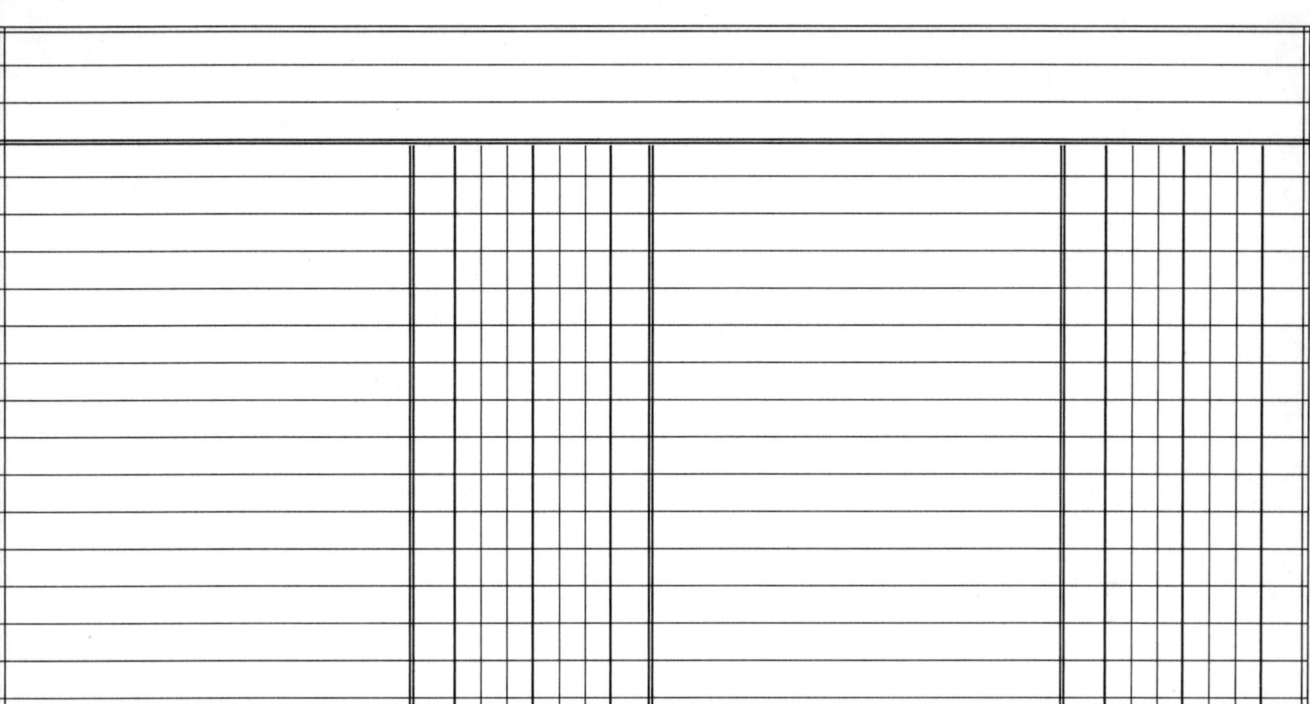

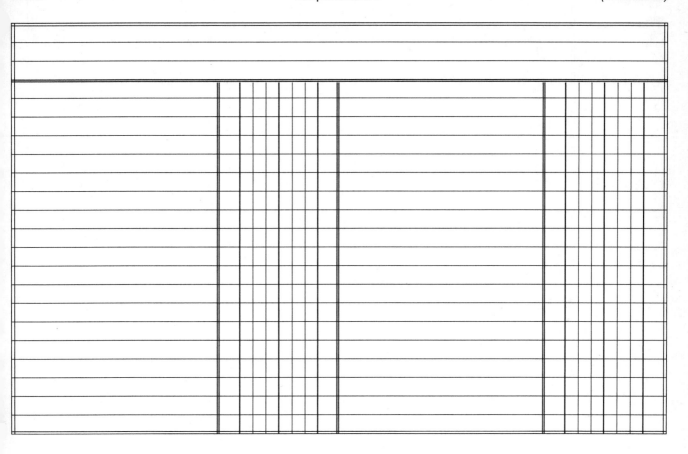

Requirements 4 a. – c.

NAME
SECTION
DATE

P1-6B

Requirement 1

Analysis of Transactions

DATE	ASSETS				= LIABILITIES + OWNER'S EQUITY		
	CASH	Account receiveable	supplies	Furniture computers	Account payable	capital	TYPE OF OWNER'S EQUITY TRANSACTION
	5000	6000		48000	16000	43000	
a.	8000					8000	investment
b.	3600					3600	revenue.
c.	-16000				-16000		
d			4000		4000		
e	4000	-4000					
f		32000				32000	Revenue
g	(4000)					(3600 4200	

NAME
SECTION
DATE

P1-6B
(Continued)

Requirement 2

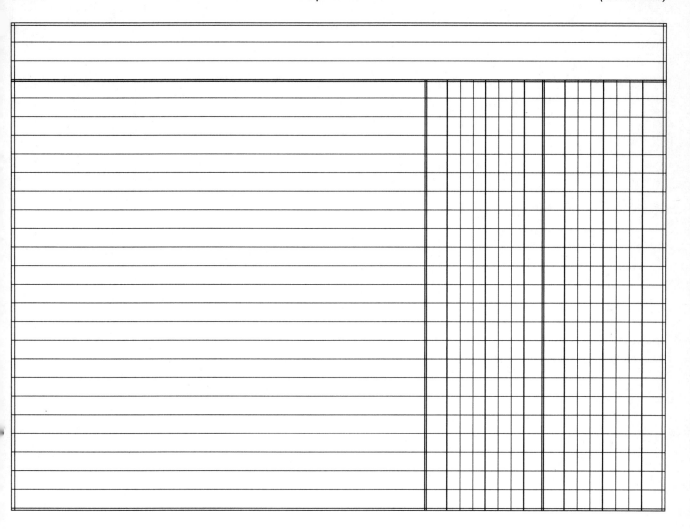

Requirement 3

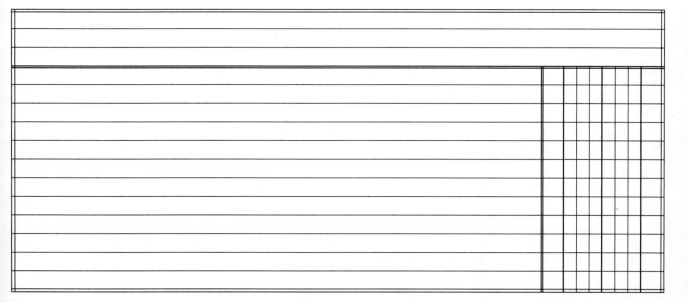

NAME
SECTION
DATE

P1-6B
(Continued)

Requirement 4

NAME
SECTION
DATE

P1-7B

May 1

May 3

May 5

May 10

May 18

May 22

May 25

May 28

May 31

NAME
SECTION
DATE

P1-8B

Requirement 1

NAME
SECTION
DATE

Requirement 2

P1-8B
(Continued)

Analysis of Transactions

DATE			ASSETS			= LIABILITIES + OWNER'S EQUITY		
								TYPE OF OWNER'S EQUITY TRANSACTION

NAME
SECTION
DATE

P1-8B
(Continued)

Requirement 3

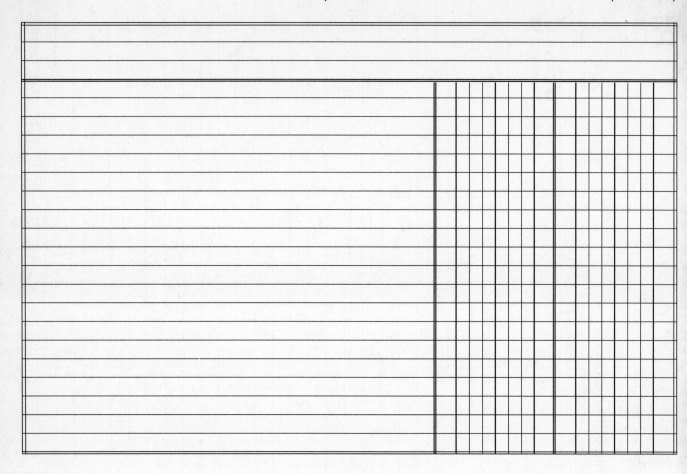

Requirement 4

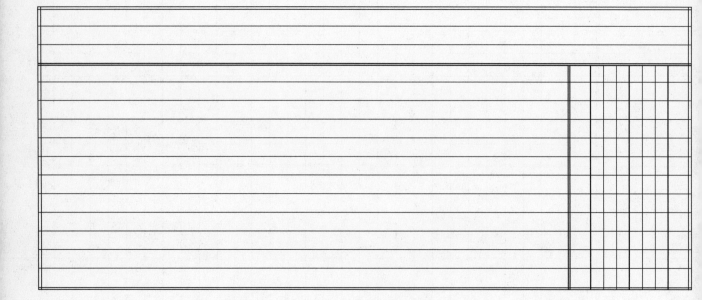

NAME
SECTION
DATE

P1-8B
(Continued)

Requirement 5

Requirement 6

NAME
SECTION
DATE

P1-1C

NAME
SECTION
DATE

P1-2C

NAME
SECTION
DATE

Decision Problem 1

Requirements 1 & 2

NAME
SECTION
DATE

Decision Problem 2

Requirements 1 & 2

NAME
SECTION
DATE

Financial Statement Problem 1

Requirements 1 – 5

NAME
SECTION
DATE

Chapter 2

E2-1

E2-2

Requirements 1 – 4

NAME
SECTION
DATE

E2-2
(Continued)

NAME
SECTION
DATE

E2-3

NAME
SECTION
DATE

E2-3
(Continued)

NAME
SECTION
DATE

E2-4

Requirements 1 & 2

Requirements 1 & 2 (Continued)

Requirement 3

NAME
SECTION
DATE

E2-5

Journal

DATE		ACCOUNT TITLES AND EXPLANATION	POST REF.	DEBIT	CREDIT

NAME
SECTION
DATE

E2-6

Requirement 1

NAME
SECTION
DATE

Requirement 1 (Continued)

Requirement 2

ACCOUNT	DEBIT	CREDIT

NAME
SECTION
DATE

E2-7
(Continued)

Requirement 1

NAME
SECTION
DATE

Requirement 2

E2-7
(Continued)

Journal

DATE		ACCOUNT TITLES AND EXPLANATION	POST REF.	DEBIT	CREDIT

NAME
SECTION
DATE

E2-7
(Continued)

Requirements 2 & 3

Account:					Account No.
Date	Item	Jrnl. Ref.	Debit	Credit	Balance

Account:					Account No.
Date	Item	Jrnl. Ref.	Debit	Credit	Balance

Account:					Account No.
Date	Item	Jrnl. Ref.	Debit	Credit	Balance

Account:					Account No.
Date	Item	Jrnl. Ref.	Debit	Credit	Balance

Account:					Account No.
Date	Item	Jrnl. Ref.	Debit	Credit	Balance

NAME
SECTION
DATE

Requirements 2 & 3 (Continued)

E2-7
(Continued)

Account:					Account No.
Date	Item	Jrnl. Ref.	Debit	Credit	Balance

Account:					Account No.
Date	Item	Jrnl. Ref.	Debit	Credit	Balance

Account:					Account No.
Date	Item	Jrnl. Ref.	Debit	Credit	Balance

Account:					Account No.
Date	Item	Jrnl. Ref.	Debit	Credit	Balance

Account:					Account No.
Date	Item	Jrnl. Ref.	Debit	Credit	Balance

NAME
SECTION
DATE

E2-7
(Continued)

Requirement 3

ACCOUNT	DEBIT	CREDIT

NAME
SECTION
DATE

E2-8

Journal				
DATE	ACCOUNT TITLES AND EXPLANATION	POST REF.	DEBIT	CREDIT

E2-9

ACCOUNT	DEBIT	CREDIT

NAME
SECTION
DATE

E2-10

ACCOUNT	DEBIT	CREDIT

NAME
SECTION
DATE

E2-11

ACCOUNT	DEBIT	CREDIT

Computations:

NAME
SECTION
DATE

E2-12

NAME
SECTION
DATE

E2-12
(Continued)

E2-13

ACCOUNT	DEBIT	CREDIT

NAME
SECTION
DATE

E2-14

Requirements 1 & 2

Requirement 3

NAME
SECTION
DATE

E2-15

Requirements 1 & 3

Requirements 1 & 3 (Continued)

NAME
SECTION
DATE

Requirement 2

E2-15
(Continued)

Journal

DATE		ACCOUNT TITLES AND EXPLANATION	POST REF.	DEBIT	CREDIT

NAME
SECTION
DATE

Requirement 4

E2-15
(Continued)

ACCOUNT	DEBIT	CREDIT

NAME
SECTION
DATE

E2-16

a. Net income for the month of March

b. Total cash paid during March

NAME
SECTION
DATE

E2-16
(Continued)

c. Cash collections from customers during March

d. Cash paid on a note payable during March

NAME
SECTION
DATE

E2-17

Requirement 1

a. ______________________________

b. ______________________________

c. ______________________________

d. ______________________________

e. ______________________________

Requirement 2

EFFECT ON TRIAL BALANCE	ACCOUNT(S) MISSTATED

NAME
SECTION
DATE

Beyond the Numbers 2-1

BALANCE SHEET ACCOUNTS

INCOME STATEMENT ACCOUNTS

NAME
SECTION
DATE

Ethical Issue

NAME
SECTION
DATE

P2-1A

NAME
SECTION
DATE

P2-2A

Requirement 1

NAME
SECTION
DATE

P2-2A
(Continued)

Requirement 1 (Continued)

NAME
SECTION
DATE

P2-2A
(Continued)

Requirement 2

Journal

DATE		ACCOUNT TITLES AND EXPLANATION	POST REF.	DEBIT	CREDIT

NAME
SECTION
DATE

P2-3A

Requirement 1

Journal				
DATE	ACCOUNT TITLES AND EXPLANATION	POST REF.	DEBIT	CREDIT

NAME
SECTION
DATE

Requirement 1 (Continued)

P2-3A
(Continued)

Journal

DATE		ACCOUNT TITLES AND EXPLANATION	POST REF.	DEBIT	CREDIT

Requirement 2

NAME
SECTION
DATE

P2-3A
(Continued)

Requirement 3

ACCOUNT	DEBIT	CREDIT

Requirement 4

dr A cr | L | O/E
+ | − | − | + | − | +

NAME
SECTION
DATE

P2-4A

Requirement 1

Journal

Page 6

DATE		ACCOUNT TITLES AND EXPLANATION	POST REF.	DEBIT	CREDIT
Nov	16	Cash		8000	
		received on account			8000
Nov	17	Account Receivable		4200	
		Service Revenue			4200
Nov	21	Account Payable		5200	
		Cash			5200
	22	Supplies		1200	
		Account payable			1200
	23	Conive Withdraw		4200	
		Cash			4200
	24	Not a bussiness transaction			
	26	Cash		3800	
		Revenue			3800
		Expence		4800	
		Cash			4800

NAME
SECTION
DATE

P2-4A

(Continued)

Requirement 2

Account: Cash | Account No.

Date		Item	Jrnl. Ref.	Debit	Credit	Balance
	16			8000		
	21					
	23					
	26			3800		
	30					

Account: | Account No.

Date		Item	Jrnl. Ref.	Debit	Credit	Balance

Account: | Account No.

Date		Item	Jrnl. Ref.	Debit	Credit	Balance

NAME
SECTION
DATE

P2-4A
(Continued)

Requirement 2 (Continued)

Account:					Account No.
Date	Item	Jrnl. Ref.	Debit	Credit	Balance

Account:					Account No.
Date	Item	Jrnl. Ref.	Debit	Credit	Balance

Account:					Account No.
Date	Item	Jrnl. Ref.	Debit	Credit	Balance

Account:					Account No.
Date	Item	Jrnl. Ref.	Debit	Credit	Balance

NAME
SECTION
DATE

P2-4A
(Continued)

Requirement 2 (Continued)

Account:					Account No.
Date	Item	Jrnl. Ref.	Debit	Credit	Balance

Account:					Account No.
Date	Item	Jrnl. Ref.	Debit	Credit	Balance

Account:					Account No.
Date	Item	Jrnl. Ref.	Debit	Credit	Balance

NAME
SECTION
DATE

Requirement 3

P2-4A
(Continued)

ACCT. NO.	ACCOUNT	DEBIT	CREDIT

NAME
SECTION
DATE

P2-5A

Requirement 1

ACCOUNT	DEBIT	CREDIT

Requirement 2

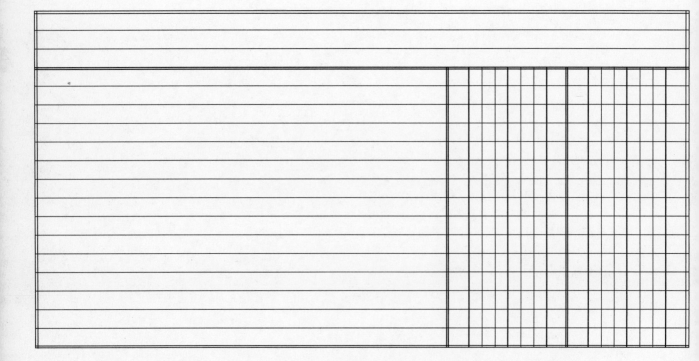

NAME
SECTION
DATE

P2-6A

Requirements 1 & 2

NAME
SECTION
DATE

Requirements 1 & 2 (Continued)

P2-6A
(Continued

NAME
SECTION
DATE

P2-6A

(Continued)

Requirement 3

ACCOUNT	DEBIT	CREDIT

NAME
SECTION
DATE

P2-7A

Requirement 1

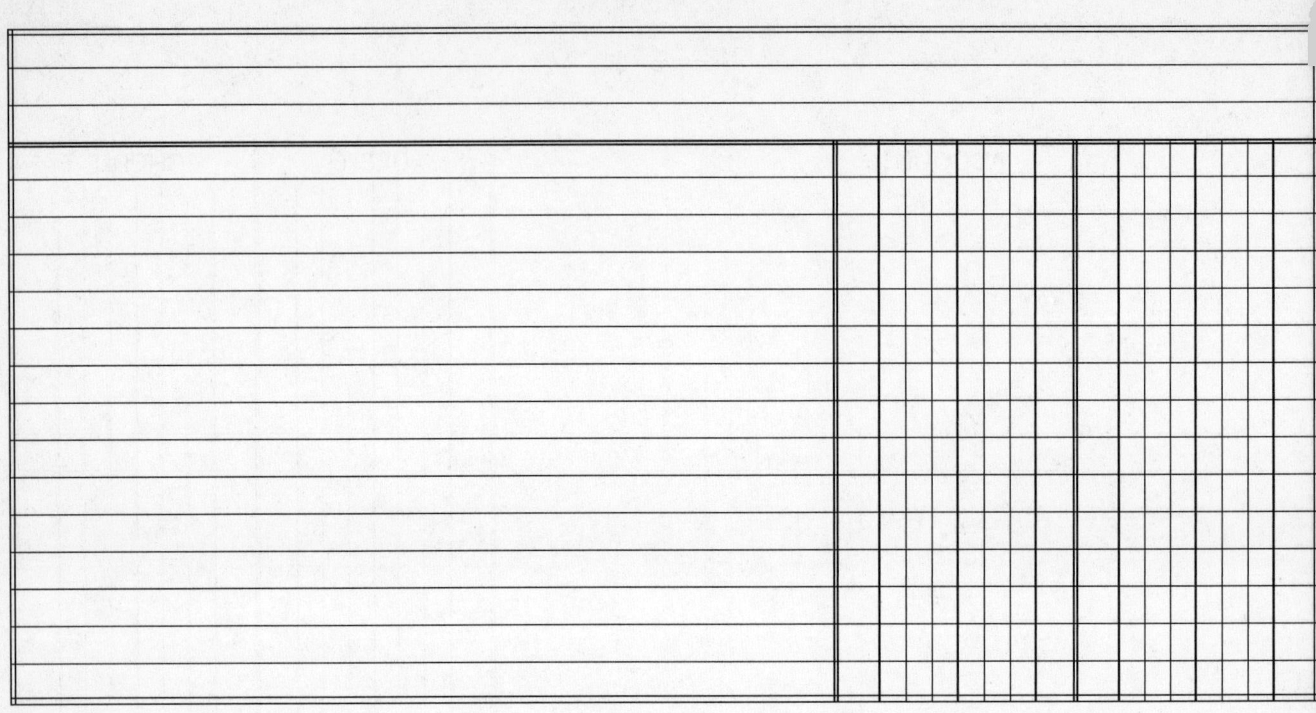

Requirement 2

NAME
SECTION
DATE

Requirement 3

P2-7A
(Continued)

NAME
SECTION
DATE

P2-8A

Journal

DATE		ACCOUNT TITLES AND EXPLANATION	POST REF.	DEBIT	CREDIT

NAME
SECTION
DATE

P2-9A

Journal

DATE		ACCOUNT TITLES AND EXPLANATION	POST REF.	DEBIT	CREDIT

NAME
SECTION
DATE

P2-1B

NAME
SECTION
DATE

P2-2B

Requirement 1

NAME
SECTION
DATE

Requirement 1 (Continued)

P2-2B
(Continued)

NAME
SECTION
DATE

P2-2B

Requirement 2

Journal

DATE	ACCOUNT TITLES AND EXPLANATION	POST REF.	DEBIT	CREDIT

NAME
SECTION
DATE

P2-3B

Requirement 1

Journal

DATE		ACCOUNT TITLES AND EXPLANATION	POST REF.	DEBIT	CREDIT

Journal

DATE		ACCOUNT TITLES AND EXPLANATION	POST REF.	DEBIT	CREDIT

NAME
SECTION
DATE

Requirement 2

P2-3B
(Continued)

NAME
SECTION
DATE

Requirement 3

P2-3B
(Continued)

ACCOUNT	DEBIT	CREDIT

NAME
SECTION
DATE

P2-4B

Requirement 1

Journal

P. 3

DATE		ACCOUNT TITLES AND EXPLANATION	POST REF.	DEBIT	CREDIT
Feb	15	Cash		6000	
		Account Receiveable			6000
	16	Account Receivable		5800	
		Revenue			5800
	20	Account Payable		3200	
		Cash			3200
	21	Supply		200	
		Account payable			200
	21	Withdraw O/E		2000	
		Cash			2000
	21	not a business transaction			
	22	Cash		6200	
		revenue			6200
	28	Pay Salary		3200	
		Cash			3200

NAME
SECTION
DATE

P2-4B
(Continued)

Requirement 2

Account: Cash **Account No.**

Date		Item	Jrnl. Ref.	Debit	Credit	Balance	
	14	Bal		4000		4000	Dr
	15			6000		10000	Dr
	20				3200	6800	Dr
	21				2000	4800	Dr
	22			6200		11000	Dr
	28				3200	7800	Dr

Account: Account receivable **Account No.**

Date		Item	Jrnl. Ref.	Debit	Credit	Balance	
	14	Bal				16000	Dr
	15				6000	10000	Dr
	16			5800		15800	Dr

Account: Supplies **Account No.**

Date		Item	Jrnl. Ref.	Debit	Credit	Balance	
	14	Bal	✓			1600	Dr
	21			200		1800	Dr

NAME
SECTION
DATE

Requirement 2 (Continued)

P2-4B
(Continued)

Account: Automobile — Account No.

Date		Item	Jrnl. Ref.	Debit	Credit	Balance	
	14	bal	✓	37200		37200	Dr

Account: Account Payable — Account No.

Date		Item	Jrnl. Ref.	Debit	Credit	Balance	
	14	bal				6000	Cr
	20			3200		2800	Cr
	21				200	3000	Cr

Account: R-Sanchez. Capital. — Account No.

Date		Item	Jrnl. Ref.	Debit	Credit	Balance	
	14	bal	✓			50000	Cr

Account: R. SanChez . Withdraw — Account No.

Date		Item	Jrnl. Ref.	Debit	Credit	Balance	
	14	bal	✓			2400	Dr
	21			2000		4400	Dr

NAME
SECTION
DATE

P2-4B
(Continued)

Requirement 2 (Continued)

Account: Service Revenue — Account No.

Date		Item	Jrnl. Ref.	Debit	Credit	Balance
	14	bal	✓		~~14~~400	14400 Cr
	16				5800	20200 Cr
	22				6200	26400 Cr

Account: Rent expens — Account No.

Date		Item	Jrnl. Ref.	Debit	Credit	Balance
	14	bal	✓			2000 Dr

Account: Salary expense — Account No.

Date		Item	Jrnl. Ref.	Debit	Credit	Balance
	14	bal	✓			7200 Dr
	28			3200		~~1000 Dr~~
						10400 Dr

NAME
SECTION
DATE

Requirement 3

P2-4B
(Continued)

Sanchez Designs Trial Balance Februrry 28 2006			
ACCT. NO.	**ACCOUNT**	**DEBIT**	**CREDIT**
1100	Cash	7800	
1200	Account recivable	15800	
1300	Supplies	1800	
1600	Automobile	37200	
2000	Accounts payable		3000
3000	R. — Capital		50000
3100	R. — withdraw	4400	
5000	Service revenue		26400
6100	Rent expense	2000	
6200	Salary expense	10400	

NAME
SECTION
DATE

P2-5B

Requirement 1

ACCOUNT	DEBIT	CREDIT

Requirement 2

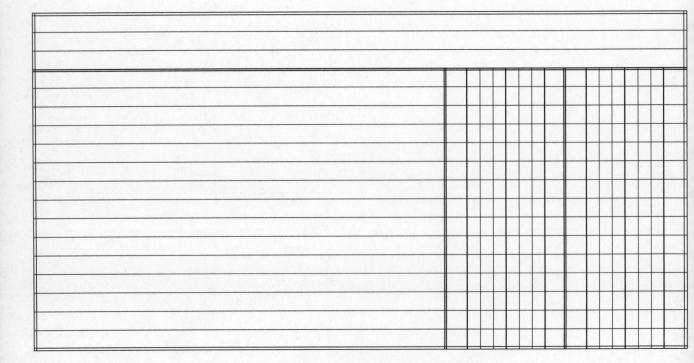

NAME
SECTION
DATE

P2-6B

Requirements 1 & 2

NAME
SECTION
DATE

Requirements 1 & 2 (Continued)

P2-6B
(Continued)

NAME
SECTION
DATE

Requirement 3

P2-6B
(Continued)

ACCOUNT	DEBIT	CREDIT

NAME
SECTION
DATE

P2-7B

Requirement 1

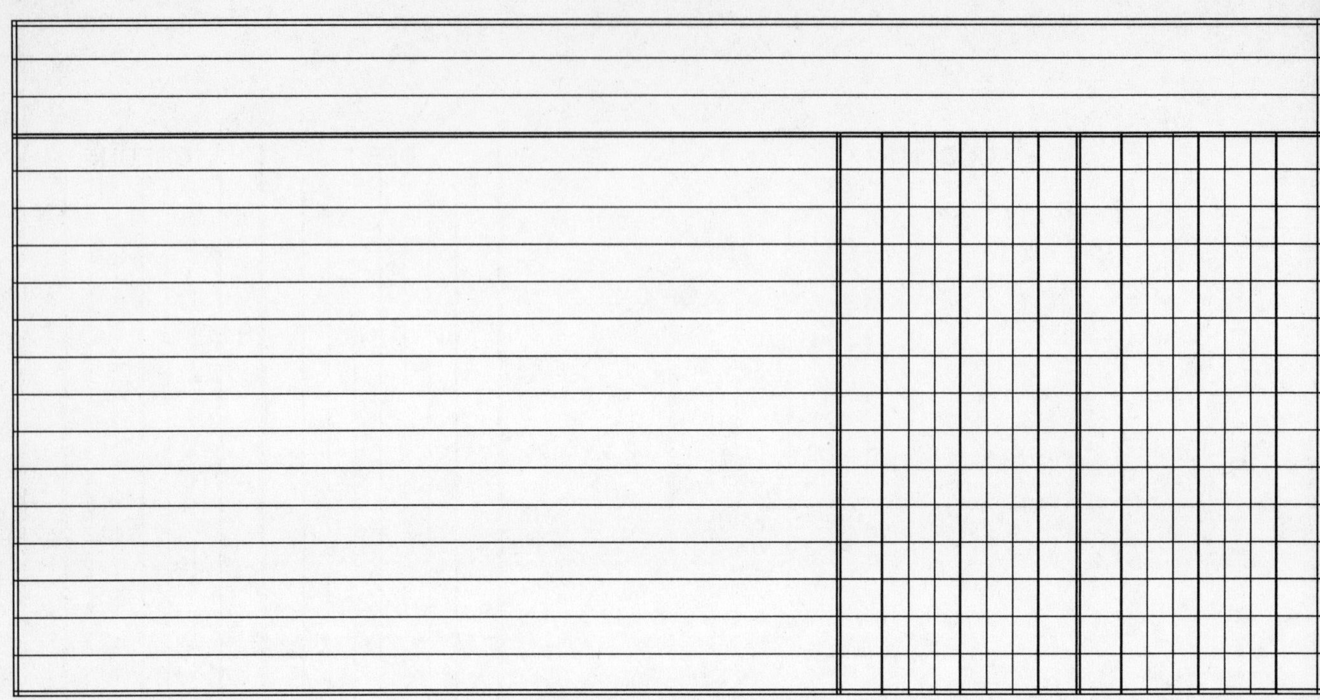

Requirement 2

NAME
SECTION
DATE

P2-7B
(Continued)

Requirement 3

NAME
SECTION
DATE

P2-8B

Journal

DATE		ACCOUNT TITLES AND EXPLANATION	POST REF.	DEBIT	CREDIT

NAME
SECTION
DATE

P2-9B

Journal

DATE		ACCOUNT TITLES AND EXPLANATION	POST REF.	DEBIT	CREDIT

NAME
SECTION
DATE

P2-1C

Requirements 1 & 2

NAME
SECTION
DATE

P2-2C

NAME
SECTION
DATE

Decision Problem 1

Requirements 1 & 2

NAME
SECTION
DATE

Decision Problem 1

(Continued)

Requirements 1 & 2 (Continued)

NAME
SECTION
DATE

Decision Problem 1

(Continued)

Requirement 3

ACCOUNT	DEBIT	CREDIT

NAME
SECTION
DATE

Decision Problem 1

(Continued)

Requirement 4

NAME
SECTION
DATE

Decision Problem 2

Requirements 1 – 3

NAME
SECTION
DATE

Financial Statement Problem

Journal

DATE		ACCOUNT TITLES AND EXPLANATION	POST REF.	DEBIT	CREDIT

NAME
SECTION
DATE

Chapter 3

E3-1

Sheridan Lake Lodge—Amount of Revenue or Expense for January

Date	Cash Basis	Accrual Basis

E3-2

a. – d.

E3-3

Requirement 1

Requirement 2

NAME
SECTION
DATE

E3-4

E3-5

	1	2	3	4

Journal

DATE		ACCOUNT TITLES AND EXPLANATION	POST REF.	DEBIT	CREDIT

E3-6

Journal

DATE		ACCOUNT TITLES AND EXPLANATION	POST REF.	DEBIT	CREDIT

E3-7

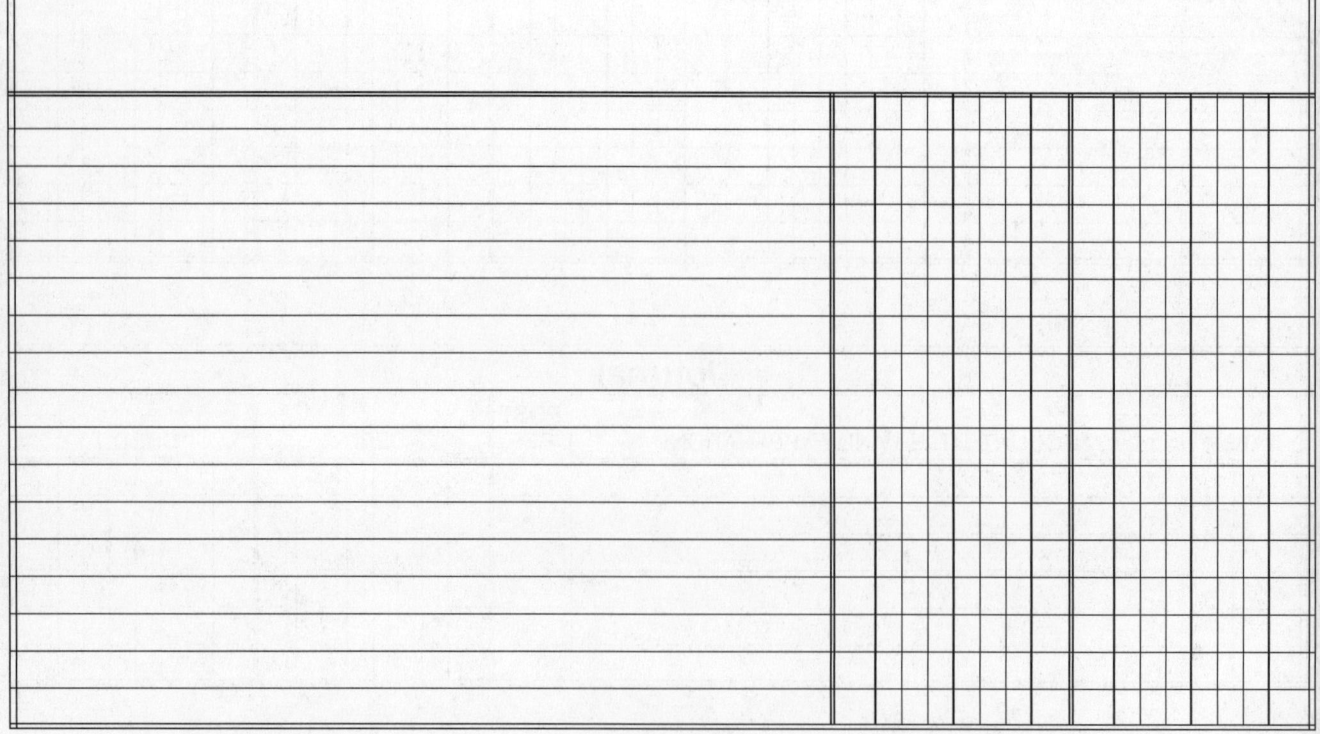

NAME
SECTION
DATE

E3-8

a. – g.

Journal

DATE		ACCOUNT TITLES AND EXPLANATION	POST REF.	DEBIT	CREDIT

NAME
SECTION
DATE

E3-9

NAME
SECTION
DATE

E3-10

Journal

DATE		ACCOUNT TITLES AND EXPLANATION	POST REF.	DEBIT	CREDIT

NAME
SECTION
DATE

E3-11

Morton Consulting						
Preparation of Adjusted Trial Balance						
May 31, 2006						
ACCOUNT TITLE	TRIAL BALANCE		ADJUSTMENTS		ADJUSTED TRIAL BALANCE	
	DEBIT	CREDIT	DEBIT	CREDIT	DEBIT	CREDIT
Cash	18000				18000	
Accounts receivable	39000				42600	
Supplies	6240				4800	
Office furniture	193800				193800	
Accumulated amortization—office furniture		84240				86400
Salary payable		0				5400
Unearned revenue		5400				4140
T. Morton, capital		158160				158160
T. Morton, withdrawals	36000				36000	
Service revenue		69780				76640
Salary expense	16140				21540	
Rent expense	8400				8400	
Amortization expense—office furniture	0				2160	
Supplies expense	0				1440	
	317580	317580			328740	328740

NAME
SECTION
DATE

E3-12

Journal

DATE		ACCOUNT TITLES AND EXPLANATION	POST REF.	DEBIT	CREDIT

NAME
SECTION
DATE

E3-13

NAME
SECTION
DATE

E3-14

Note: If needed, create a second dollar-column for assets.

NAME
SECTION
DATE

E3-15

Requirement 1

Requirement 2

E3-16

Requirement 1

Requirement 2

AME
ECTION
ATE

E3-17

Requirements 1, 3, & 6

NAME
SECTION
DATE

Requirements 1, 3, & 6 (Continued)

E3-1
(Continue

AME
ECTION
ATE

Requirement 2

E3-17
(Continued)

Journal

DATE		ACCOUNT TITLES AND EXPLANATION	POST REF.	DEBIT	CREDIT

NAME
SECTION
DATE

E3-17
(Continued)

Requirements 4 & 5

ACCOUNT TITLE	TRIAL BALANCE		ADJUSTMENTS		ADJUSTED TRIAL BALANCE	
	DEBIT	CREDIT	DEBIT	CREDIT	DEBIT	CREDIT

AME
ECTION
ATE

Requirement 6

E3-17

(Continued)

Journal

DATE		ACCOUNT TITLES AND EXPLANATION	POST REF.	DEBIT	CREDIT

NAME
SECTION
DATE

Requirement 7

E3-17
(Continued)

AME
ECTION
ATE

Requirement 7 (Continued)

E3-17
(Continued)

NOTE: If needed, create a second dollar-column for assets.

NAME
SECTION
DATE

E3-18

NAME
SECTION
DATE

E3-18

(Continued)

NAME
SECTION
DATE

E3-19

NAME
SECTION
DATE

E3-19

(Continued)

NAME
SECTION
DATE

Beyond the Numbers 3-1

AME
ECTION
ATE

Ethical Issue

Requirements 1 – 3

NAME
SECTION
DATE

P3-1A

Requirements 1 & 2

Amount of Revenue or Expense for March

Date	Cash Basis	Accrual Basis

Requirement 3

NAME
SECTION
DATE

P3-2A

NAME
SECTION
DATE

P3-3A

Journal

DATE		ACCOUNT TITLES AND EXPLANATION	POST REF.	DEBIT	CREDIT

NAME
SECTION
DATE

P3-3A
(Continued)

Journal					
DATE		ACCOUNT TITLES AND EXPLANATION	POST REF.	DEBIT	CREDIT

Computations:

NAME
SECTION
DATE

P3-4A

Journal

DATE		ACCOUNT TITLES AND EXPLANATION	POST REF.	DEBIT	CREDIT

AME
ECTION
ATE

P3-5A

Requirements 1 & 2

NAME
SECTION
DATE

Requirement 2

P3-5A
(Continued)

Journal

DATE		ACCOUNT TITLES AND EXPLANATION	POST REF.	DEBIT	CREDIT

NAME
SECTION
DATE

P3-5A

(Continued)

Requirement 3

ACCOUNT	DEBIT	CREDIT

Requirement 4

NAME
SECTION
DATE

P3-6A

Requirement 1

Belford System Income Statement For the year End Dec 31 06		
Revenue		
Service revenue.		374730
Expense :		
Ne		

Belford System Statement of Owner's equity For the year end Dec 31 2006	
T. Belford Capital Jan 1 2006	
Add: Net income	
Less withdrawn	
T. Belford Capital Dec 31 2006	

NAME
SECTION
DATE

Requirement 1 (Continued)

P3-6A
(Continued)

Belford System Balance Sheet Dec 31 2006			
Assets		Liabilities	
Cash			
Account Receivable			
Supplies			
Prepaid Rent			
Equipment			
Less A-A			
Office furniture			
less A A			
Total Assets			

Note: If needed, create a second dollar-column for assets.

NAME
SECTION
DATE

Requirements 1 & 2

P3-6A
(Continued)

NAME
SECTION
DATE

P3-7A

Requirement 1

ACCOUNT TITLE	TRIAL BALANCE		ADJUSTMENTS		ADJUSTED TRIAL BALANCE	
	DEBIT	CREDIT	DEBIT	CREDIT	DEBIT	CREDIT

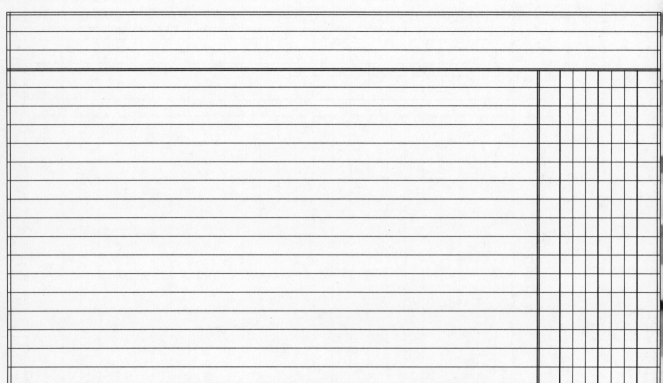

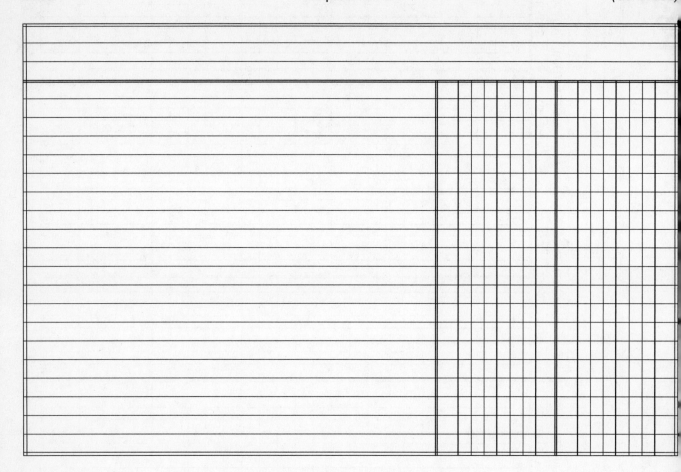

NAME
SECTION
DATE

Requirement 2

P3-7A
(Continued)

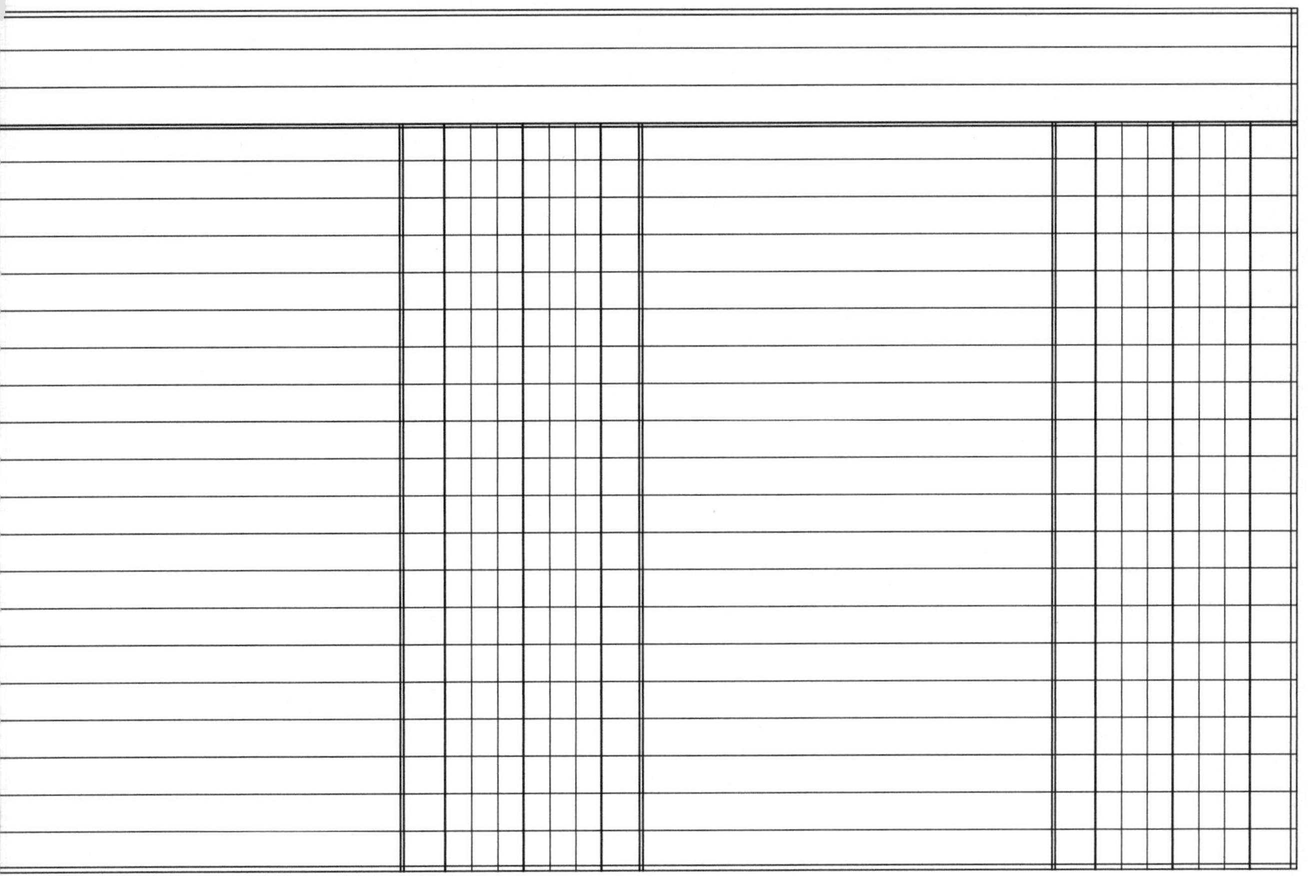

Note: If needed, create a second dollar-column for assets.

NAME
SECTION
DATE

P3-8A

Requirement 1

Journal

DATE		ACCOUNT TITLES AND EXPLANATION	POST REF.	DEBIT	CREDIT

NAME
SECTION
DATE

Requirement 2

P3-8A
(Continued)

NAME
SECTION
DATE

Requirement 3

P3-8A
(Continued)

NAME
SECTION
DATE

P3-1B

Requirements 1 & 2

Amount of Revenue or Expense for October		
Date	Cash Basis	Accrual Basis

Requirement 3

NAME
SECTION
DATE

P3-2B

NAME
SECTION
DATE

P3-3B

Journal

DATE		ACCOUNT TITLES AND EXPLANATION	POST REF.	DEBIT	CREDIT

NAME
SECTION
DATE

P3-3B

(Continued)

Journal

DATE		ACCOUNT TITLES AND EXPLANATION	POST REF.	DEBIT	CREDIT

Computations:

NAME
SECTION
DATE

P3-4B

Journal

DATE		ACCOUNT TITLES AND EXPLANATION	POST REF.	DEBIT	CREDIT

NAME
SECTION
DATE

P3-5B

Requirements 1 & 2

NAME
SECTION
DATE

Requirement 2

P3-5B
(Continued)

Journal

DATE		ACCOUNT TITLES AND EXPLANATION	POST REF.	DEBIT	CREDIT

NAME
SECTION
DATE

P3-5B
(Continued)

Requirement 3

ACCOUNT	DEBIT	CREDIT

Requirement 4

AME
ECTION
ATE

P3-6B

NAME
SECTION
DATE

P3-6B
(Continued)

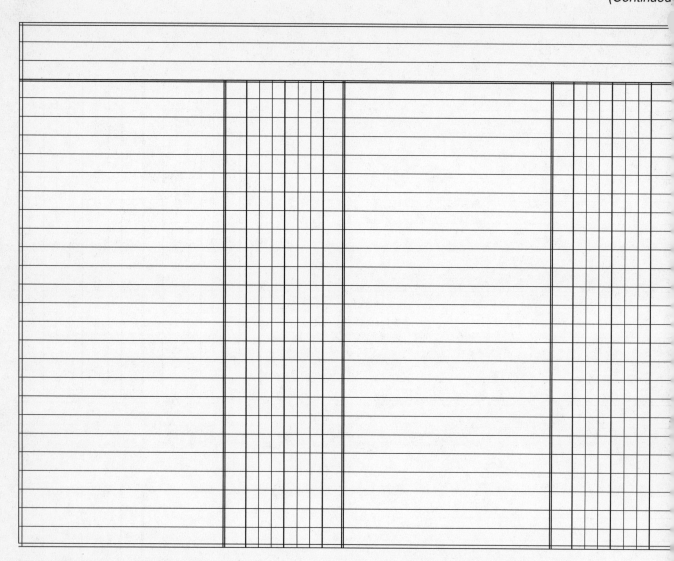

Note: If needed, create a second dollar-column for assets.

NAME
SECTION
DATE

Requirements 1 & 2

P3-6B
(Continued)

NAME
SECTION
DATE

P3-7B

Requirement 1

ACCOUNT TITLE	TRIAL BALANCE		ADJUSTMENTS		ADJUSTED TRIAL BALANCE	
	DEBIT	CREDIT	DEBIT	CREDIT	DEBIT	CREDIT

NAME
SECTION
DATE

Requirement 2

P3-7B
(Continued)

NAME
SECTION
DATE

P3-7B

Requirement 2 (Continued)

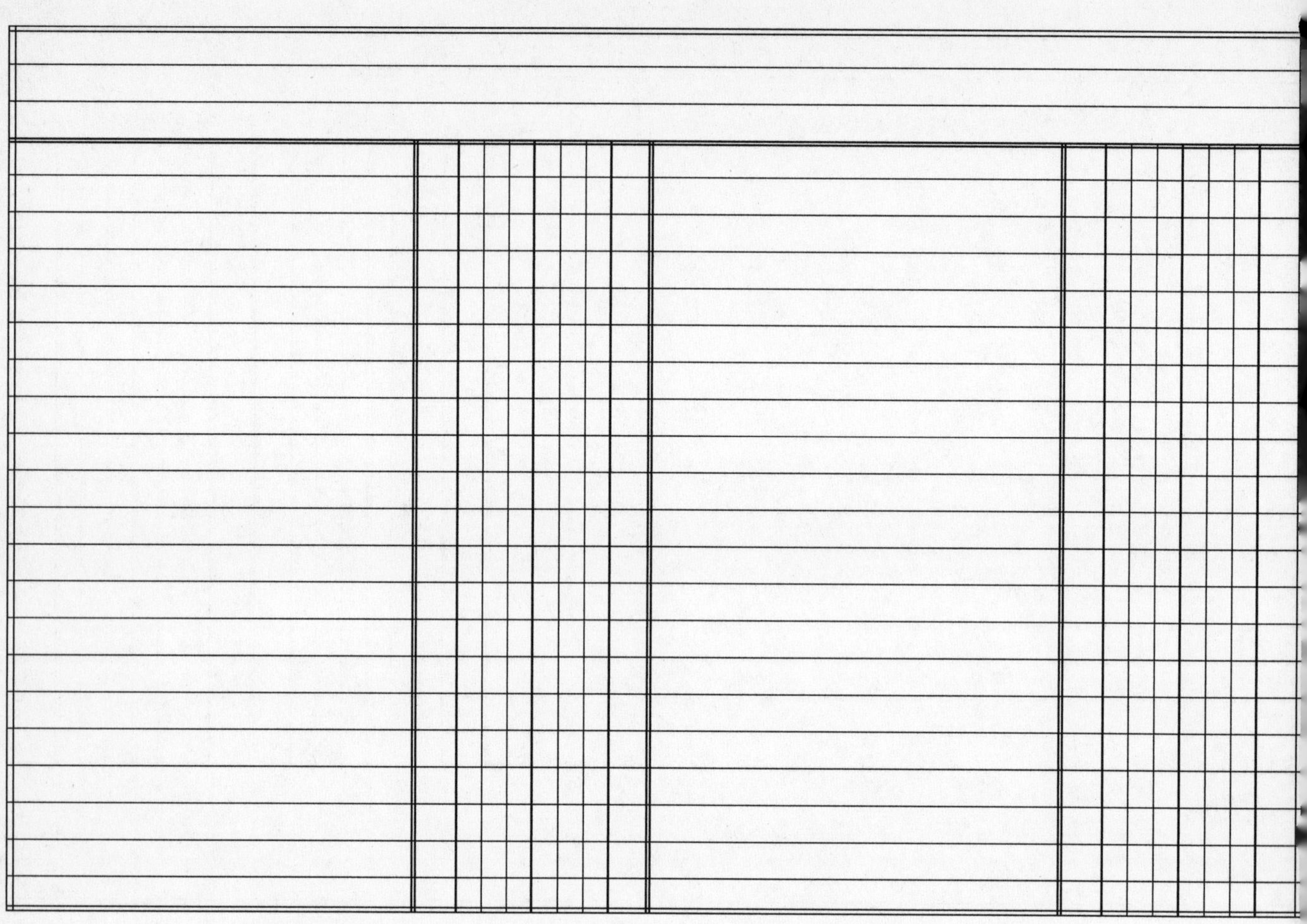

Note: If needed, created a second dollar-column for assets.

AME
ECTION
ATE

P3-8B

Requirement 1

Journal

DATE		ACCOUNT TITLES AND EXPLANATION	POST REF.	DEBIT	CREDIT

NAME
SECTION
DATE

Requirement 2

P3-8B
(Continued)

NAME
SECTION
DATE

Requirement 3

P3-8B
(Continued)

NAME
SECTION
DATE

P3-1C

AME
ECTION
ATE

P3-2C

Requirement 1

Requirement 2

NAME
SECTION
DATE

Decision Problem 1

Requirement 1

Requirement 2

NAME
SECTION
DATE

Decision Problem 1

(Continued)

Requirement 3

Requirement 4

NAME
SECTION
DATE

Decision Problem 2

Requirements 1–3

NAME
SECTION
DATE

Financial Statement Problem

Requirements 1–3

Requirement 2

Journal				
DATE	ACCOUNT TITLES AND EXPLANATION	POST REF.	DEBIT	CREDIT

NAME
SECTION
DATE

Financial Statement Problem

(Continued)

Requirement 3

NAME
SECTION
DATE

E3A-1

Requirement 1

Requirement 2

Requirement 3

NAME
SECTION
DATE

E3A-2

Requirement 1

Journal				
DATE	ACCOUNT TITLES AND EXPLANATION	POST REF.	DEBIT	CREDIT

NAME
SECTION
DATE

E3A-2
(Continued)

Requirement 2

Journal

DATE		ACCOUNT TITLES AND EXPLANATION	POST REF.	DEBIT	CREDIT

Requirement 3

NAME
SECTION
DATE

P3A-1

Requirement 1

Journal

DATE		ACCOUNT TITLES AND EXPLANATION	POST REF.	DEBIT	CREDIT

Requirement 2

Journal

DATE		ACCOUNT TITLES AND EXPLANATION	POST REF.	DEBIT	CREDIT

NAME
SECTION
DATE

P3A-1
(Continued)

Requirement 3

Account:					Account No.
Date	Item	Jrnl. Ref.	Debit	Credit	Balance

Account:					Account No.
Date	Item	Jrnl. Ref.	Debit	Credit	Balance

Account:					Account No.
Date	Item	Jrnl. Ref.	Debit	Credit	Balance

Account:					Account No.
Date	Item	Jrnl. Ref.	Debit	Credit	Balance

NAME
SECTION
DATE

Requirement 4

P3A-1
(Continued)

Journal

DATE		ACCOUNT TITLES AND EXPLANATION	POST REF.	DEBIT	CREDIT

NAME
SECTION
DATE

P3A-1
(Continued)

Requirement 4 (Continued)

Account:						Account No.
Date		Item	Jrnl. Ref.	Debit	Credit	Balance

Account:						Account No.
Date		Item	Jrnl. Ref.	Debit	Credit	Balance

Account:						Account No.
Date		Item	Jrnl. Ref.	Debit	Credit	Balance

Account:						Account No.
Date		Item	Jrnl. Ref.	Debit	Credit	Balance

Requirement 5

NAME
SECTION
DATE

P3A-2

Requirements 1 & 2

Journal				
DATE	ACCOUNT TITLES AND EXPLANATION	POST REF.	DEBIT	CREDIT

NAME
SECTION
DATE

Requirement 3

P3A-2

(Continued)

NAME
SECTION
DATE

Chapter 4

E4-1

The foldout work sheet to solve this problem can be found in the back of the book.

E4-2

Journal

DATE		ACCOUNT TITLES AND EXPLANATION	POST REF.	DEBIT	CREDIT

NAME
SECTION
DATE

E4-3

NAME
SECTION
DATE

E4-3
(Continued)

NAME
SECTION
DATE

E4-4

ACCOUNT	DEBIT	CREDIT

E4-5

Journal

DATE	ACCOUNT TITLES AND EXPLANATION	POST REF.	DEBIT	CREDIT

NAME
SECTION
DATE

E4-6

Journal

DATE		ACCOUNT TITLES AND EXPLANATION	POST REF.	DEBIT	CREDIT

NAME
SECTION
DATE

E4-7

Requirement 1

Journal

DATE		ACCOUNT TITLES AND EXPLANATION	POST REF.	DEBIT	CREDIT

NAME
SECTION
DATE

E4-8

NAME
SECTION
DATE

E4-9

Journal

DATE		ACCOUNT TITLES AND EXPLANATION	POST REF.	DEBIT	CREDIT

NAme
SECTION
DATE

E4-10

Parts 1 – 3

Journal				
DATE	ACCOUNT TITLES AND EXPLANATION	POST REF.	DEBIT	CREDIT

NAME
SECTION
DATE

E4-11

Requirement 1

NAME
SECTION
DATE

E4-11
(Continued)

Requirement 2

E4-12

Journal

DATE		ACCOUNT TITLES AND EXPLANATION	POST REF.	DEBIT	CREDIT

NAME
SECTION
DATE

E4-13

Requirements 1 & 2

NAME
SECTION
DATE

E4-14

Requirement 1

Journal				
DATE	ACCOUNT TITLES AND EXPLANATION	POST REF.	DEBIT	CREDIT

NAME
SECTION
DATE

Requirement 1

E4-14
(Continued)

NAME
SECTION
DATE

E4-14
(Continued)

Requirement 2

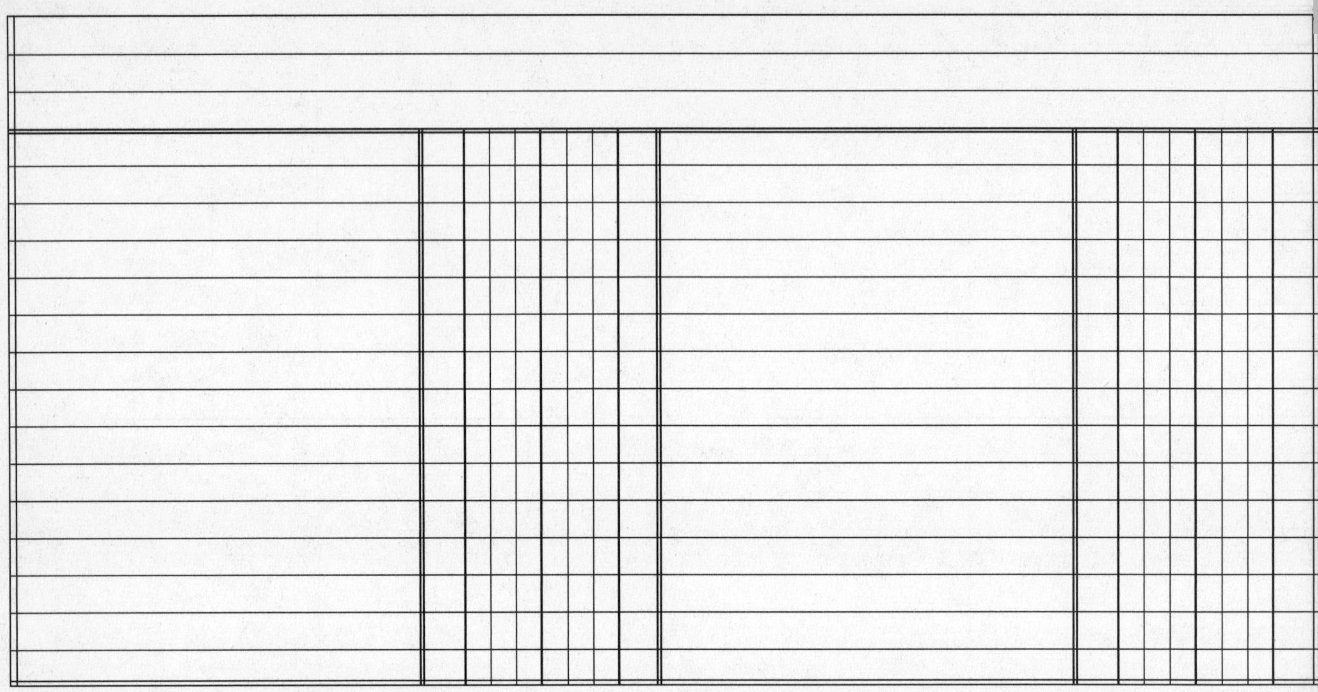

Note: If needed, create a second dollar-column for assets.

Requirement 3

COMPUTATIONS:

Requirement 4

The foldout work sheet to solve this problem can be found in the back of the book.

NAME
SECTION
DATE

E4-15

Part 1

NAME
SECTION
DATE

E4-15
(Continued)

Part 2

Part 3

NAME
SECTION
DATE

E4-15
(Continued)

Part 4

Part 5

NAME
SECTION
DATE

Requirements 1 – 3

Ethical Issue

P4-1A

The foldout work sheet to solve this problem can be found in the back of the book.

NAME
SECTION
DATE

P4-2A

Requirement 1

Journal

DATE		ACCOUNT TITLES AND EXPLANATION	POST REF.	DEBIT	CREDIT

NAME
SECTION
DATE

Requirement 1 (Continued)

P4-2A
(Continued)

Journal

DATE		ACCOUNT TITLES AND EXPLANATION	POST REF.	DEBIT	CREDIT

NAME
SECTION
DATE

Requirement 2

P4-2A
(Continued)

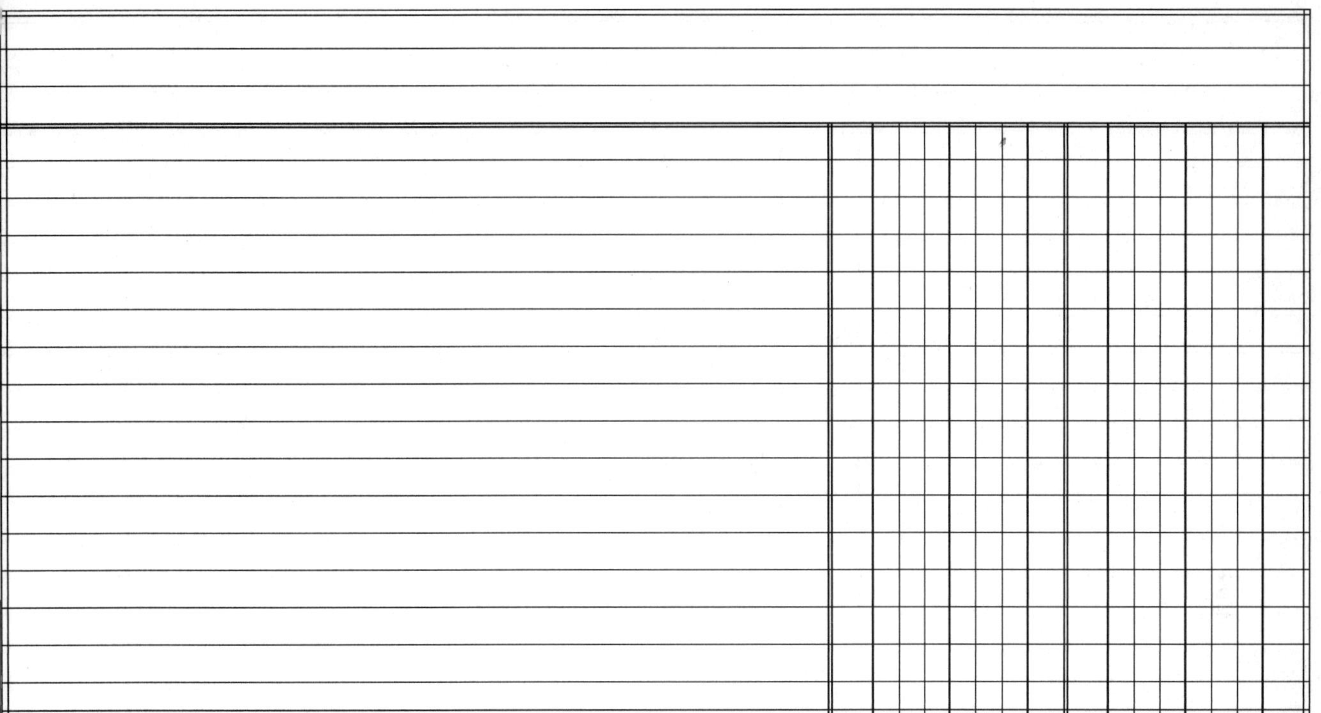

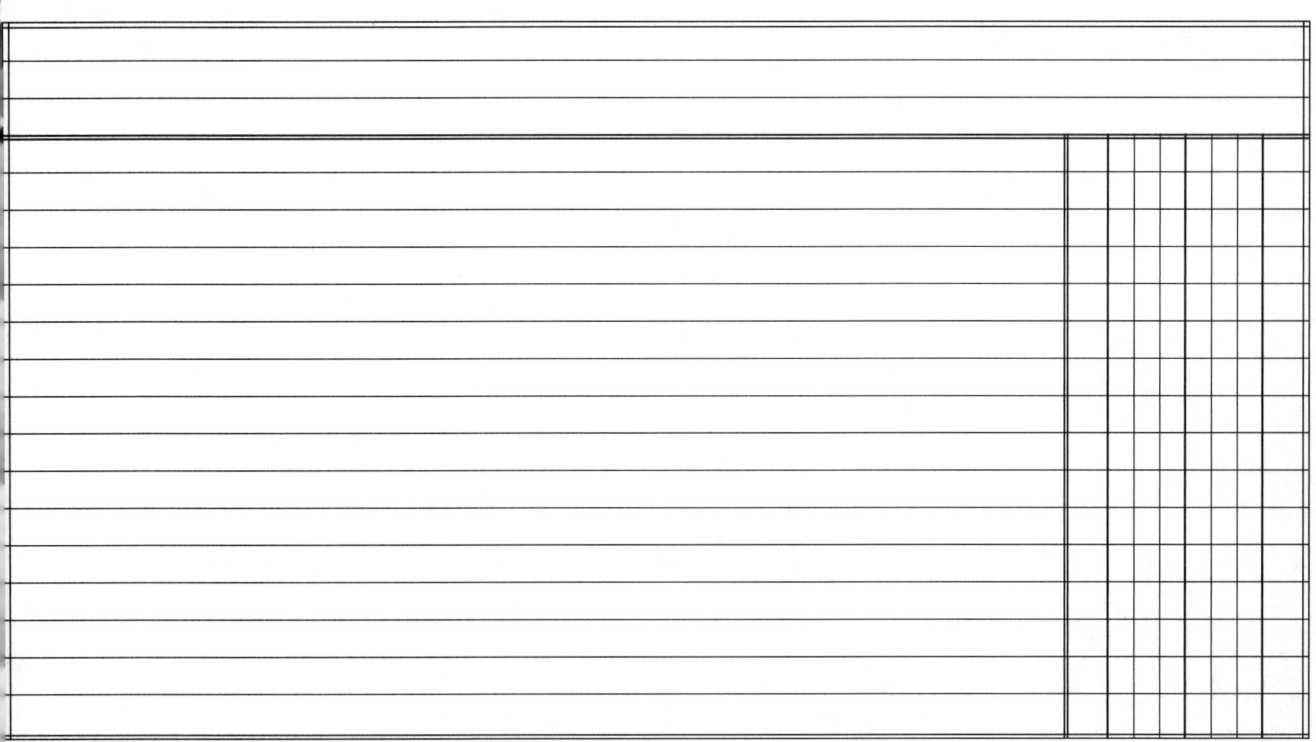

NAME
SECTION
DATE

P4-2A
(Continued)

Requirement 2 (Continued)

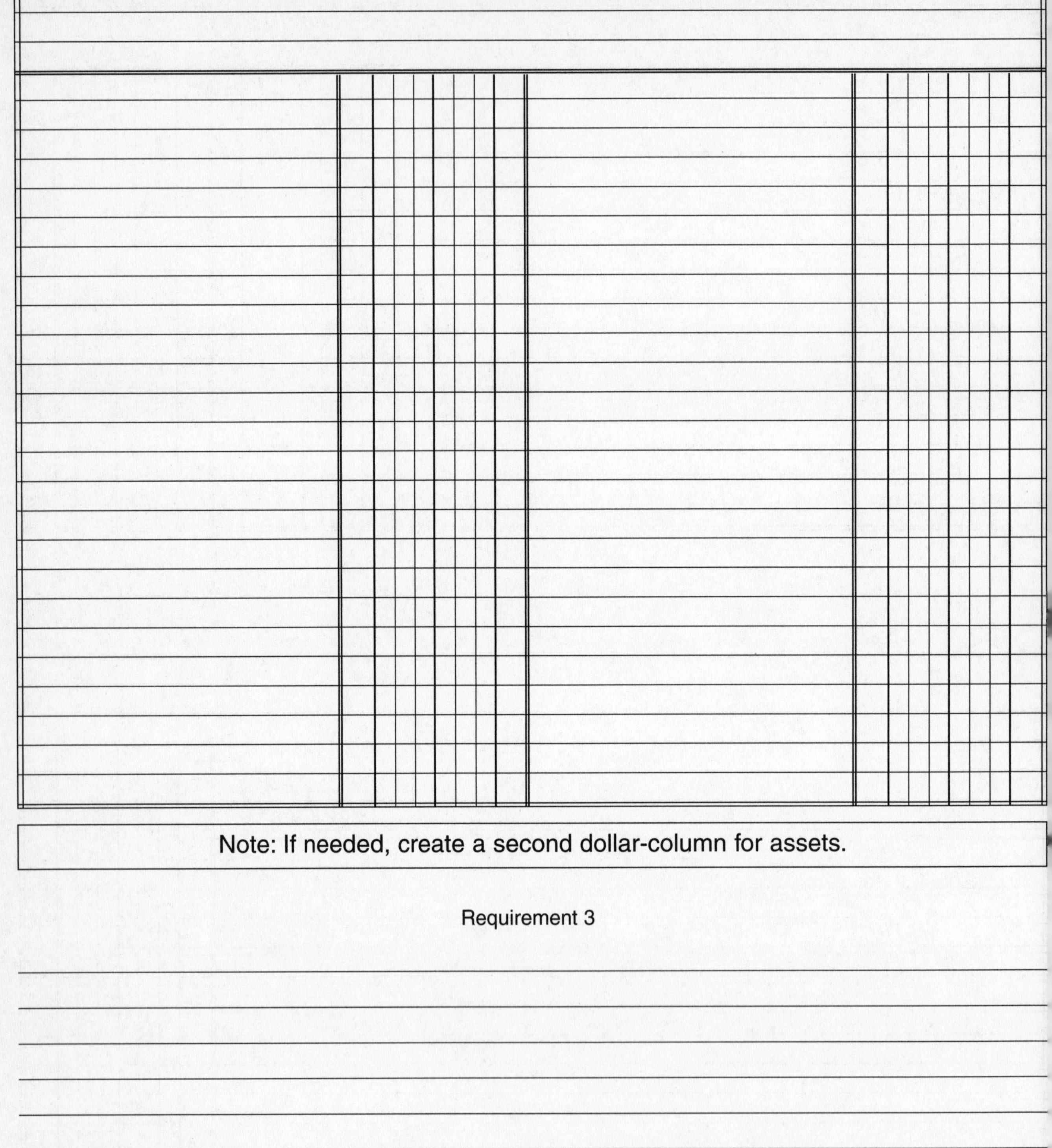

Note: If needed, create a second dollar-column for assets.

Requirement 3

NAME
SECTION
DATE

P4-3A

Requirement 1

The foldout work sheet to solve this problem can be found in the back of the book.

Requirement 2

NAME
SECTION
DATE

Requirement 2 (Continued)

P4-3A
(Continued)

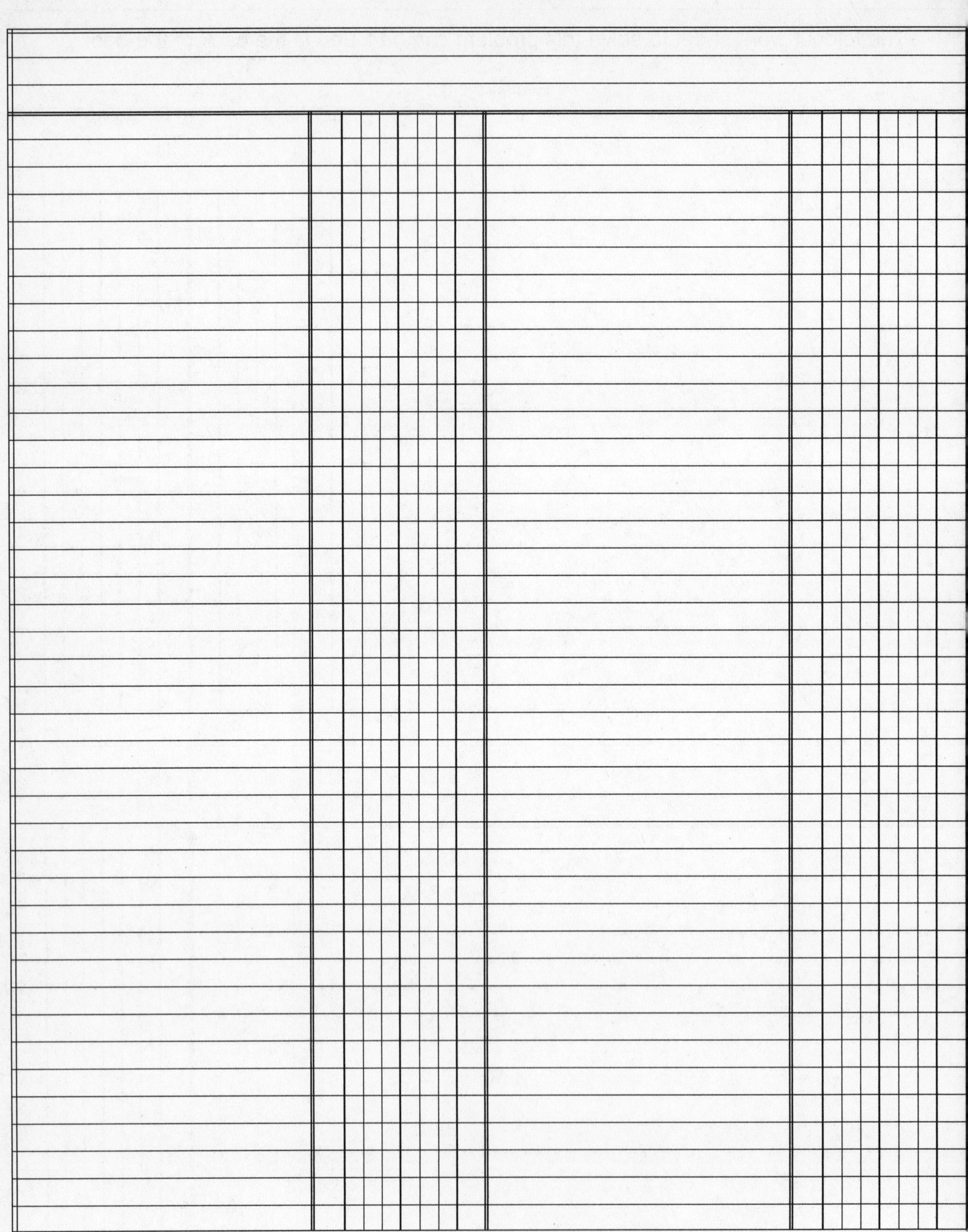

Note: If needed, create a second dollar-column for assets.

NAME
SECTION
DATE

Requirement 3

P4-3A
(Continued)

Journal

DATE		ACCOUNT TITLES AND EXPLANATION	POST REF.	DEBIT	CREDIT

NAME
SECTION
DATE

P4-3A
(Continued)

Requirement 3 (Continued)

Journal

DATE		DESCRIPTION	POST REF.	DEBIT	CREDIT

Requirement 4

NAME
SECTION
DATE

P4-4A

Requirement 1

NAME
SECTION
DATE

P4-4A
(Continued)

Requirement 2

ACCOUNT	DEBIT	CREDIT

NAME
SECTION
DATE

P4-5A

Requirements 1 & 4

Account:						Account No.
Date		Item	Jrnl. Ref.	Debit	Credit	Balance

Account:						Account No.
Date		Item	Jrnl. Ref.	Debit	Credit	Balance

Account:						Account No.
Date		Item	Jrnl. Ref.	Debit	Credit	Balance

Account:						Account No.
Date		Item	Jrnl. Ref.	Debit	Credit	Balance

NAME
SECTION
DATE

Requirements 1 & 4 (Continued)

P4-5A
(Continued)

Account:					Account No.
Date		Item	Jrnl. Ref.	Debit	Credit	Balance

Account:					Account No.
Date		Item	Jrnl. Ref.	Debit	Credit	Balance

Account:					Account No.
Date		Item	Jrnl. Ref.	Debit	Credit	Balance

Account:					Account No.
Date		Item	Jrnl. Ref.	Debit	Credit	Balance

Account:					Account No.
Date	Item	Jrnl. Ref.	Debit	Credit	Balance

Account:					Account No.
Date	Item	Jrnl. Ref.	Debit	Credit	Balance

Account:					Account No.
Date	Item	Jrnl. Ref.	Debit	Credit	Balance

Account:					Account No.
Date	Item	Jrnl. Ref.	Debit	Credit	Balance

NAME
SECTION
DATE

Requirements 1 & 4 (Continued)

P4-5A
(Continued)

Account: | Account No.

Date		Item	Jrnl. Ref.	Debit	Credit	Balance

Account: | Account No.

Date		Item	Jrnl. Ref.	Debit	Credit	Balance

Account: | Account No.

Date		Item	Jrnl. Ref.	Debit	Credit	Balance

Account: | Account No.

Date		Item	Jrnl. Ref.	Debit	Credit	Balance

NAME
SECTION
DATE

P4-5A
(Continued)

Requirements 1 & 4 (Continued)

Account: Account No.

Date		Item	Jrnl. Ref.	Debit	Credit	Balance

Account: Account No.

Date		Item	Jrnl. Ref.	Debit	Credit	Balance

Account: Account No.

Date		Item	Jrnl. Ref.	Debit	Credit	Balance

Account: Account No.

Date		Item	Jrnl. Ref.	Debit	Credit	Balance

NAME
SECTION
DATE

P4-5A
(Continued)

Requirements 1 & 4 (Continued)

Account:					Account No.
Date	Item	Jrnl. Ref.	Debit	Credit	Balance

Account:					Account No.
Date	Item	Jrnl. Ref.	Debit	Credit	Balance

Requirement 2

The foldout work sheet to solve this problem can be found in the back of the book.

AME
ECTION
ATE

Requirement 3

P4-5A

(Continued)

NAME
SECTION
DATE

Requirement 3 (Continued)

P4-5A
(Continued)

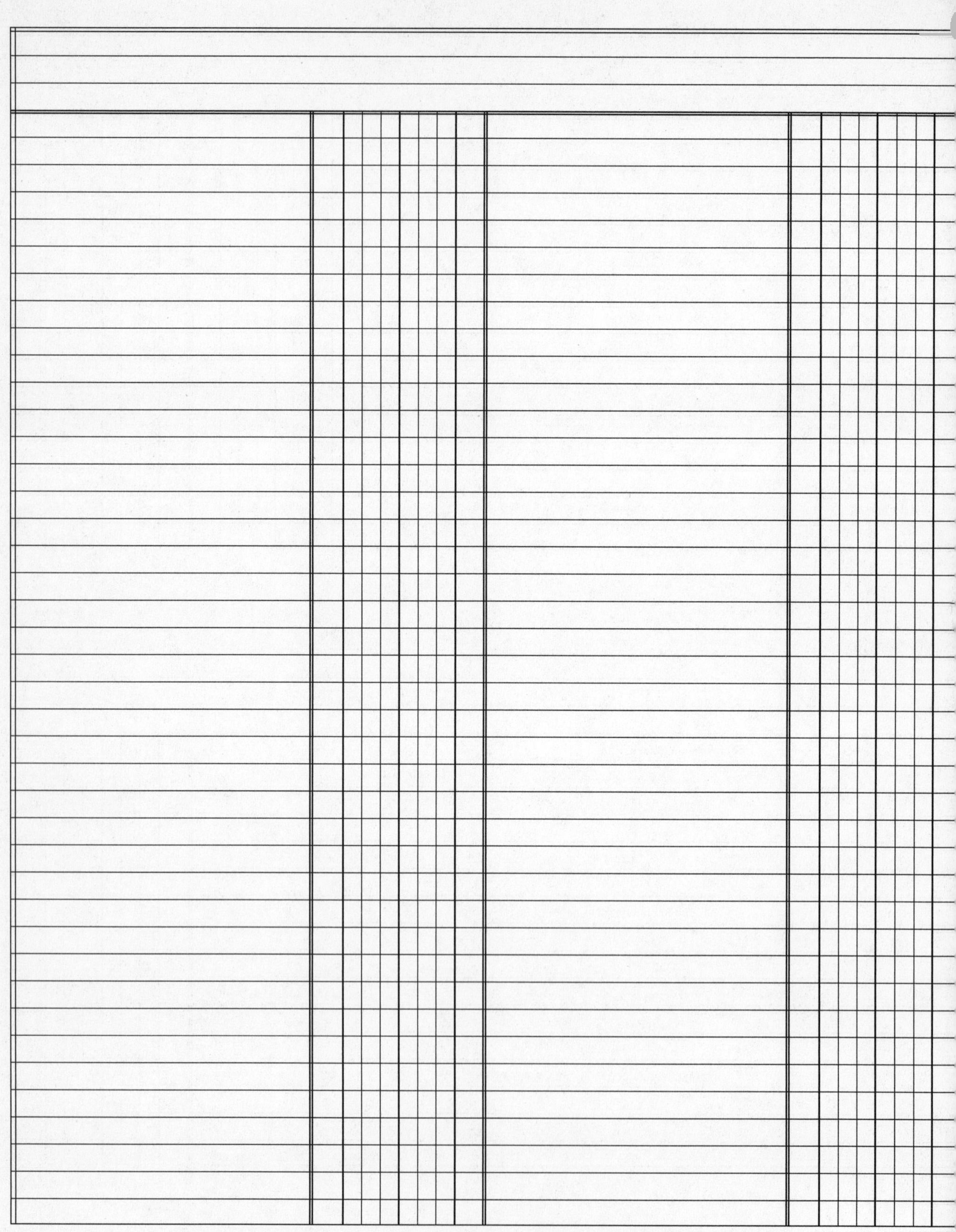

Note: If needed, create a second dollar-column for assets.

NAME
SECTION
DATE

Requirement 4

P4-5A
(Continued)

Journal

DATE		ACCOUNT TITLES AND EXPLANATION	POST REF.	DEBIT	CREDIT

NAME
SECTION
DATE

Requirement 4 (Continued)

P4-5A
(Continued)

Journal

DATE		ACCOUNT TITLES AND EXPLANATION	POST REF.	DEBIT	CREDIT

NAME
SECTION
DATE

Requirement 5

P4-5A
(Continued)

ACCOUNT	DEBIT	CREDIT

NAME
SECTION
DATE

P4-6A

Requirement 1

NAME
SECTION
DATE

Requirement 1 (Continued)

Requirement 2

Situations a – c

Situation d

P4-7A

Situation e

Journal				
DATE	ACCOUNT TITLES AND EXPLANATION	POST REF.	DEBIT	CREDIT

NAME
SECTION
DATE

P4-7A
(Continued)

Situation f

Journal

DATE		ACCOUNT TITLES AND EXPLANATION	POST REF.	DEBIT	CREDIT

NAME
SECTION
DATE

P4-8A

Requirement 1

The foldout work sheet to solve this problem can be found in the back of the book.

Requirements 2 & 3

Journal

DATE		ACCOUNT TITLES AND EXPLANATION	POST REF.	DEBIT	CREDIT

NAME
SECTION
DATE

Requirements 2 & 3

P4-8A
(Continued)

Journal

DATE		ACCOUNT TITLES AND EXPLANATION	POST REF.	DEBIT	CREDIT

NAME
SECTION
DATE

Requirement 4

P4-8A
(Continued)

ACCOUNT	DEBIT	CREDIT

NAME
SECTION
DATE

P4-9A
(Continued)

Requirement 1

The foldout work sheet to solve this problem can be found in the back of the book.

Requirement 2

Journal

DATE	ACCOUNT TITLES AND EXPLANATION	POST REF.	DEBIT	CREDIT

NAME
SECTION
DATE

Requirement 2 (Continued)

P4-9A
(Continued)

Journal

DATE		ACCOUNT TITLES AND EXPLANATION	POST REF.	DEBIT	CREDIT

NAME
SECTION
DATE

Requirement 3

P4-9A
(Continued)

NAME
SECTION
DATE

Requirement 4

P4-9A
(Continued)

CURRENT RATIO:

DEBT RATIO:

P4-1B

The foldout work sheet to solve this problem can be found in the back of the book.

NAME
SECTION
DATE

P4-2B

Requirement 1

Journal

DATE		ACCOUNT TITLES AND EXPLANATION	POST REF.	DEBIT	CREDIT

NAME
SECTION
DATE

P4-2B

(Continued)

Requirement 1 (Continued)

Journal

DATE		ACCOUNT TITLES AND EXPLANATION	POST REF.	DEBIT	CREDIT

NAME
SECTION
DATE

Requirement 2

P4-2B
(Continued)

NAME
SECTION
DATE

P4-2B
(Continued)

Requirement 2 (Continued)

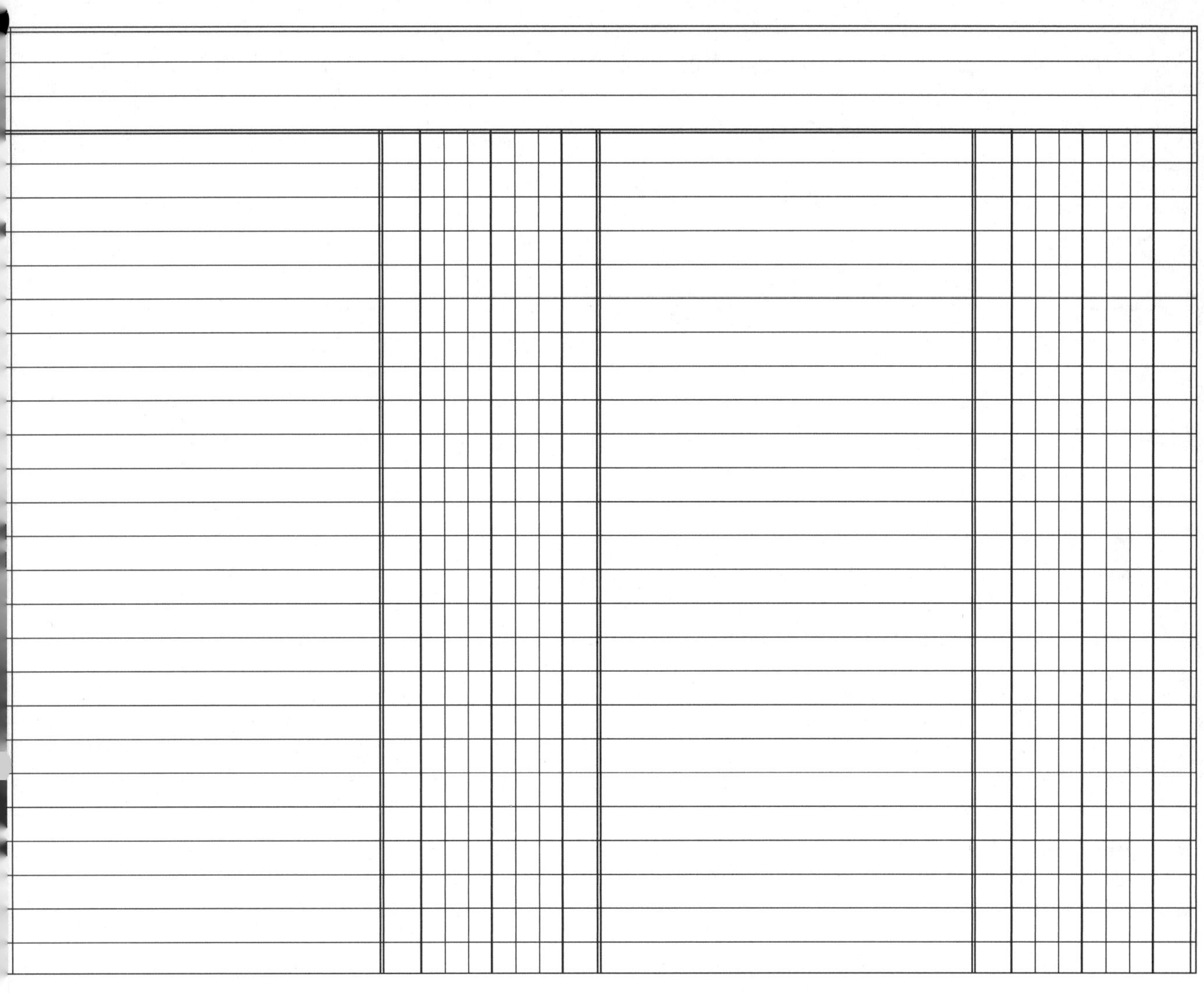

Note: If needed, create a second dollar-column for assets.

Requirement 3

NAME
SECTION
DATE

P4-3B

Requirement 1

The foldout work sheet to solve this problem can be found in the back of the book.

Requirement 2

Requirement 2 (Continued)

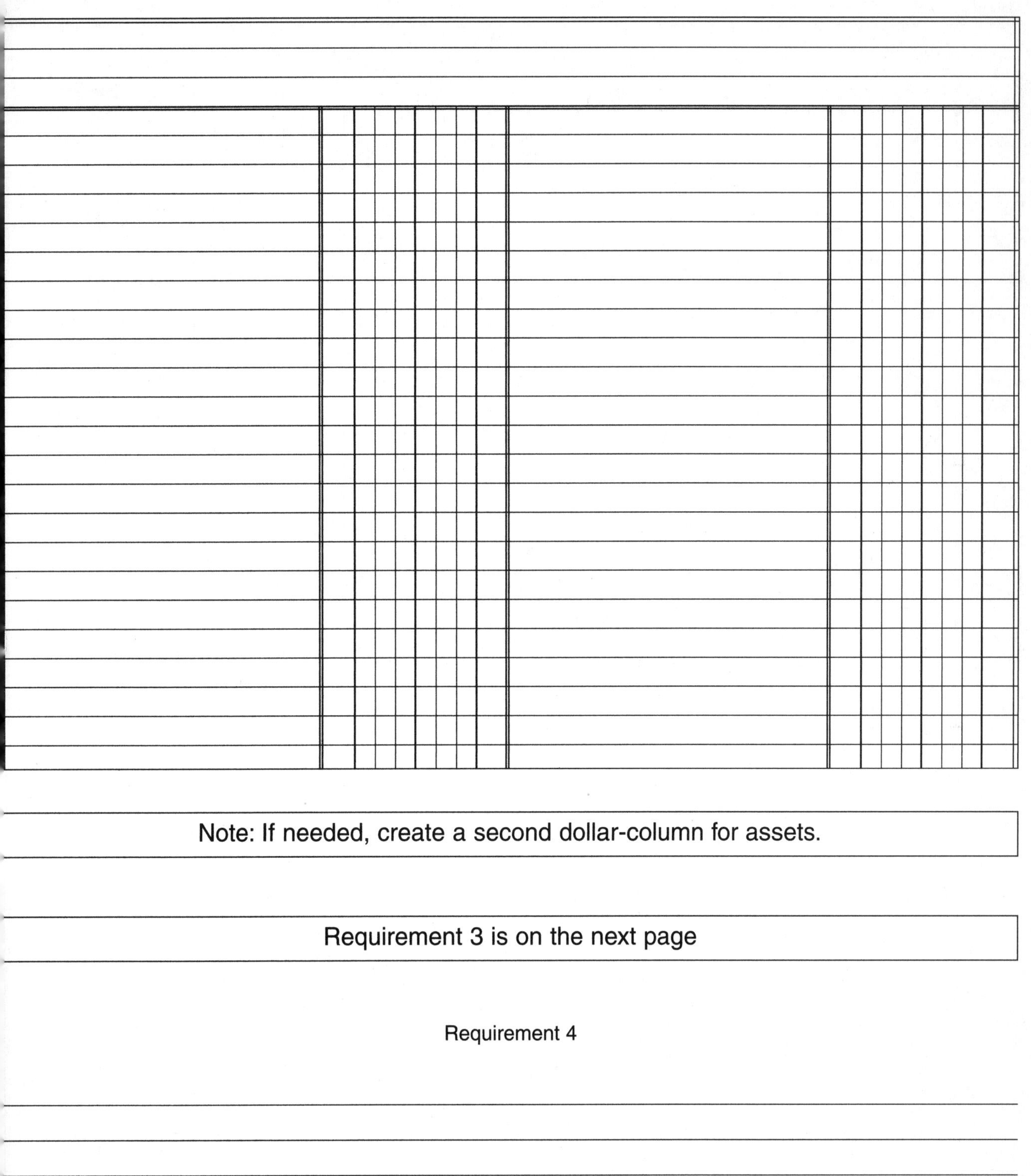

Note: If needed, create a second dollar-column for assets.

Requirement 3 is on the next page

Requirement 4

NAME
SECTION
DATE

Requirement 3

P4-3B
(Continued)

Journal

DATE		ACCOUNT TITLES AND EXPLANATION	POST REF.	DEBIT	CREDIT

NAME
SECTION
DATE

P4-4B

Requirement 1

NAME
SECTION
DATE

Requirement 2

P4-4B

(Continued)

ACCOUNT	DEBIT	CREDIT

NAME
SECTION
DATE

P4-5B

Requirements 1 & 4

Account:						Account No.
Date		Item	Jrnl. Ref.	Debit	Credit	Balance

Account:						Account No.
Date		Item	Jrnl. Ref.	Debit	Credit	Balance

Account:						Account No.
Date		Item	Jrnl. Ref.	Debit	Credit	Balance

Account:						Account No.
Date		Item	Jrnl. Ref.	Debit	Credit	Balance

NAME
SECTION
DATE

Requirements 1 & 4 (Continued)

P4-5B
(Continued)

Account:						Account No.
Date		Item	Jrnl. Ref.	Debit	Credit	Balance

Account:						Account No.
Date		Item	Jrnl. Ref.	Debit	Credit	Balance

Account:						Account No.
Date		Item	Jrnl. Ref.	Debit	Credit	Balance

Account:						Account No.
Date		Item	Jrnl. Ref.	Debit	Credit	Balance

NAME
SECTION
DATE

P4-5B
(Continued)

Requirements 1 & 4 (Continued)

Account:					Account No.
Date	Item	Jrnl. Ref.	Debit	Credit	Balance

Account:					Account No.
Date	Item	Jrnl. Ref.	Debit	Credit	Balance

Account:					Account No.
Date	Item	Jrnl. Ref.	Debit	Credit	Balance

Account:					Account No.
Date	Item	Jrnl. Ref.	Debit	Credit	Balance

NAME
SECTION
DATE

P4-5B
(Continued)

Requirements 1 & 4 (Continued)

Account:					Account No.
Date	Item	Jrnl. Ref.	Debit	Credit	Balance

Account:					Account No.
Date	Item	Jrnl. Ref.	Debit	Credit	Balance

Account:					Account No.
Date	Item	Jrnl. Ref.	Debit	Credit	Balance

Account:					Account No.
Date	Item	Jrnl. Ref.	Debit	Credit	Balance

NAME
SECTION
DATE

Requirements 1 & 4 (Continued)

P4-5B
(Continued)

Account:						Account No.
Date		Item	Jrnl. Ref.	Debit	Credit	Balance

Account:						Account No.
Date		Item	Jrnl. Ref.	Debit	Credit	Balance

Account:						Account No.
Date		Item	Jrnl. Ref.	Debit	Credit	Balance

Account:						Account No.
Date		Item	Jrnl. Ref.	Debit	Credit	Balance

NAME
SECTION
DATE

P4-5B
(Continued)

Requirements 1 & 4 (Continued)

Account: Account No.

Date		Item	Jrnl. Ref.	Debit	Credit	Balance

Account: Account No.

Date		Item	Jrnl. Ref.	Debit	Credit	Balance

Account: Account No.

Date		Item	Jrnl. Ref.	Debit	Credit	Balance

NAME
SECTION
DATE

P4-5B

(Continued)

Requirement 2

The foldout work sheet to solve this problem can be found in the back of the book.

Requirement 3

NAME
SECTION
DATE

Requirement 3 (Continued)

P4-5B
(Continued)

NAME
SECTION
DATE

P4-5B
(Continued)

Requirement 4

Journal

DATE		ACCOUNT TITLES AND EXPLANATION	POST REF.	DEBIT	CREDIT

NAME
SECTION
DATE

Requirement 4 (Continued)

P4-5B
(Continued)

Journal

DATE	ACCOUNT TITLES AND EXPLANATION	POST REF.	DEBIT	CREDIT

NAME
SECTION
DATE

P4-5B
(Continued)

Requirement 5

ACCOUNT	DEBIT	CREDIT

NAME
SECTION
DATE

P4-6B

Requirement 1

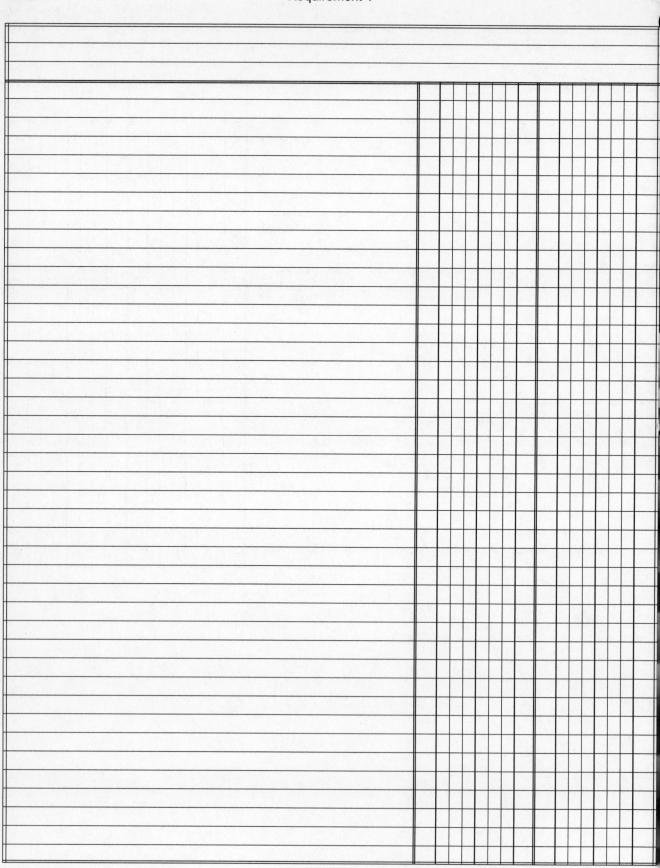

NAME
SECTION
DATE

P4-6B
(Continued)

Requirement 1 (Continued)

Requirement 2

NAME
SECTION
DATE

P4-7B

Situations a – c

Situation d

NAME
SECTION
DATE

Situation e

P4-7B
(Continued)

Journal

DATE		ACCOUNT TITLES AND EXPLANATION	POST REF.	DEBIT	CREDIT

NAME
SECTION
DATE

Situation f

P4-7B
(Continued)

Journal

DATE		ACCOUNT TITLES AND EXPLANATION	POST REF.	DEBIT	CREDIT

NAME
SECTION
DATE

P4-8B

Requirement 1

The foldout work sheet to solve this problem can be found in the back of the book.

Requirements 2 & 3

Journal

DATE		ACCOUNT TITLES AND EXPLANATION	POST REF.	DEBIT	CREDIT

NAME
SECTION
DATE

Requirements 2 & 3 (Continued)

P4-8B
(Continued)

Journal

DATE		ACCOUNT TITLES AND EXPLANATION	POST REF.	DEBIT	CREDIT

NAME
SECTION
DATE

Requirement 4

P4-8B
(Continued)

ACCOUNT	DEBIT	CREDIT

NAME
SECTION
DATE

P4-9B

Requirement 1

The foldout work sheet to solve this problem can be found in the back of the book.

Requirement 2

Journal

DATE		ACCOUNT TITLES AND EXPLANATION	POST REF.	DEBIT	CREDIT

NAME
SECTION
DATE

Requirement 3

P4-9B
(Continued)

NAME
SECTION
DATE

Requirement 4

P4-9B
(Continued)

CURRENT RATIO:

DEBT RATIO:

AME
ECTION
ATE

P4-1C

Requirement 1

Requirement 2

NAME
SECTION
DATE

P4-2C

NAME
SECTION
DATE

Decision Problem 1

NAME
SECTION
DATE

Decision Problem 1

(Continued

Note: If needed, create a second dollar-column for assets.

The foldout work sheet to solve this problem can be found in the back of the book.

AME
ECTION
ATE

Decision Problem 2

a.

b.

NAME
SECTION
DATE

Financial Statement Problem

Requirements a – f

AME
ECTION
ATE

P4A-1

Requirements 1, 2, & 3

Account:						Account No.
Date		Item	Jrnl. Ref.	Debit	Credit	Balance

Account:						Account No.
Date		Item	Jrnl. Ref.	Debit	Credit	Balance

Requirements 2 & 3

Journal

DATE		ACCOUNT TITLES AND EXPLANATION	POST REF.	DEBIT	CREDIT

NAME
SECTION
DATE

P4A-1

(Continued)

Requirement 4

Account:						Account No.
Date		Item	Jrnl. Ref.	Debit	Credit	Balance

Account:						Account No.
Date		Item	Jrnl. Ref.	Debit	Credit	Balance

Journal

DATE		ACCOUNT TITLES AND EXPLANATION	POST REF.	DEBIT	CREDIT

NAME
SECTION
DATE

NAME
SECTION
DATE

Chapter 5

E5-1

Requirement 1

Requirement 2

	2007	2006

NAME
SECTION
DATE

Requirement 3

E5-1
(Continued)

E5-2

Journal

DATE		ACCOUNT TITLES AND EXPLANATION	POST REF.	DEBIT	CREDIT

NAME
SECTION
DATE

E5-3

Journal

DATE		ACCOUNT TITLES AND EXPLANATION	POST REF.	DEBIT	CREDIT

NAME
SECTION
DATE

E5-4

Journal

DATE		ACCOUNT TITLES AND EXPLANATION	POST REF.	DEBIT	CREDIT

NAME
SECTION
DATE

E5-5

Requirements 1 – 3

Journal

DATE		ACCOUNT TITLES AND EXPLANATION	POST REF.	DEBIT	CREDIT

NAME
SECTION
DATE

E5-6

Journal

DATE		ACCOUNT TITLES AND EXPLANATION	POST REF.	DEBIT	CREDIT

NAME
SECTION
DATE

E5-7

Journal

DATE	ACCOUNT TITLES AND EXPLANATION	POST REF.	DEBIT	CREDIT

NAME
SECTION
DATE

E5-8

Requirement 1

Journal					
DATE		ACCOUNT TITLES AND EXPLANATION	POST REF.	DEBIT	CREDIT

Requirement 2

NAME
SECTION
DATE

E5-9

Journal

DATE		ACCOUNT TITLES AND EXPLANATION	POST REF.	DEBIT	CREDIT

NAME
SECTION
DATE

E5-10

E5-11

NAME
SECTION
DATE

E5-12

Requirement 1

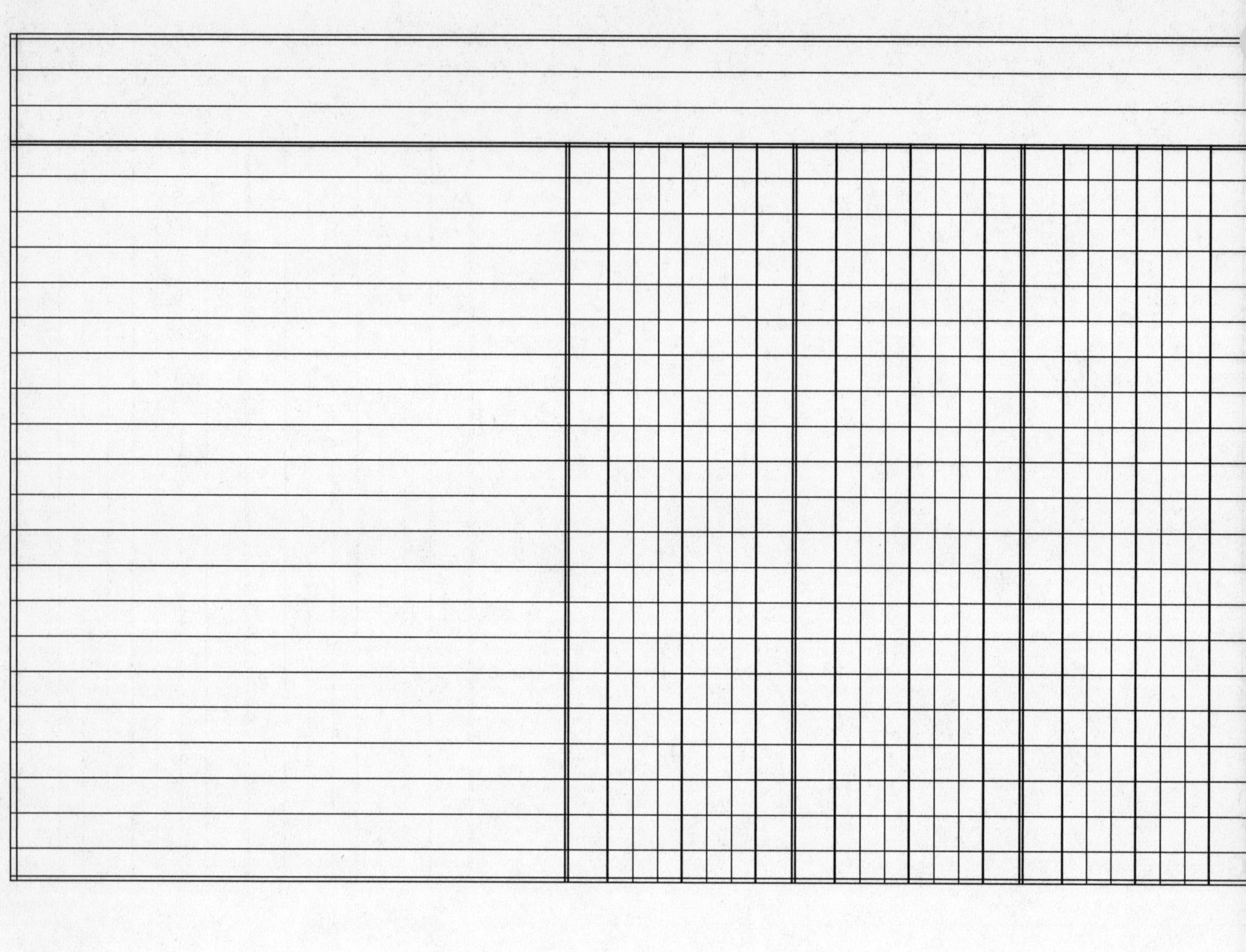

Requirement 2

Inventory Turnover:

NAME
SECTION
DATE

E5-13

Gross Margin Percentage:

NAME
SECTION
DATE

E5-14

NAME
SECTION
DATE

E5-15

Sales	Sales Discounts	Net Sales	Beginning Inventory	Net Purchases	Ending Inventory	Cost of Goods Sold	Gross Margin
$48,150	(a) ______	$46,750	$17,750	$33,350	$19,700	(b) ______	$15,350
41,200	$1,050	(c) ______	12,875	21,500	(d) ______	$22,050	(e) ______
46,750	900	45,850	(f) ______	22,450	11,300	29,700	(g) ______
(h) ______	1,500	(i) ______	20,350	(j) ______	24,115	36,250	19,300

Computations:

NAME
SECTION
DATE

E5-16

E5-17

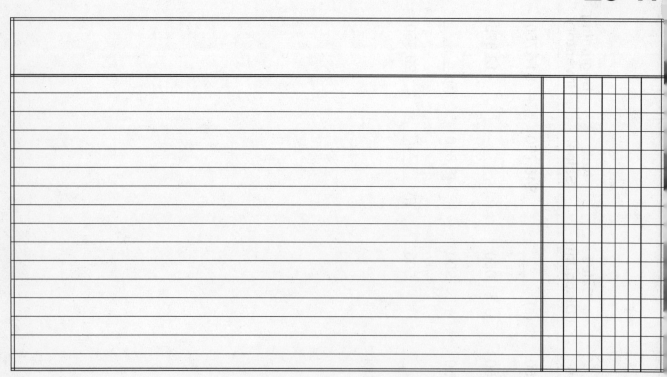

NAME
SECTION
DATE

E5-18

Requirements 1 & 2

NAME
SECTION
DATE

Requirement 2

E5-18
(Continued)

Journal

DATE		ACCOUNT TITLES AND EXPLANATION	POST REF.	DEBIT	CREDIT

NAME
SECTION
DATE

Requirement 2 (Continued)

E5-18
(Continued)

Journal

DATE		ACCOUNT TITLES AND EXPLANATION	POST REF.	DEBIT	CREDIT

NAME
SECTION
DATE

Requirement 3

E5-18
(Continued)

NAME
SECTION
DATE

Beyond the Numbers 5-1

NAME
SECTION
DATE

Ethical Issue

Requirements 1 & 2

NAME
SECTION
DATE

P5-1A

NAME
SECTION
DATE

P5-2A

Journal

DATE		ACCOUNT TITLES AND EXPLANATION	POST REF.	DEBIT	CREDIT

NAME
SECTION
DATE

P5-3A

Requirement 1

Journal				
DATE	ACCOUNT TITLES AND EXPLANATION	POST REF.	DEBIT	CREDIT

NAME
SECTION
DATE

P5-3A
(Continued)

Requirement 1 (Continued)

Journal

DATE		ACCOUNT TITLES AND EXPLANATION	POST REF.	DEBIT	CREDIT

Requirement 2

NAME
SECTION
DATE

P5-4A

The foldout work sheet to solve this problem can be found in the back of the book.

P5-5A

Requirement 1

Journal

DATE		ACCOUNT TITLES AND EXPLANATION	POST REF.	DEBIT	CREDIT

NAME
SECTION
DATE

P5-5A
(Continued)

Requirement 1 (Continued)

Journal

DATE		ACCOUNT TITLES AND EXPLANATION	POST REF.	DEBIT	CREDIT

Requirement 2

NAME
SECTION
DATE

P5-6A

Requirement 1

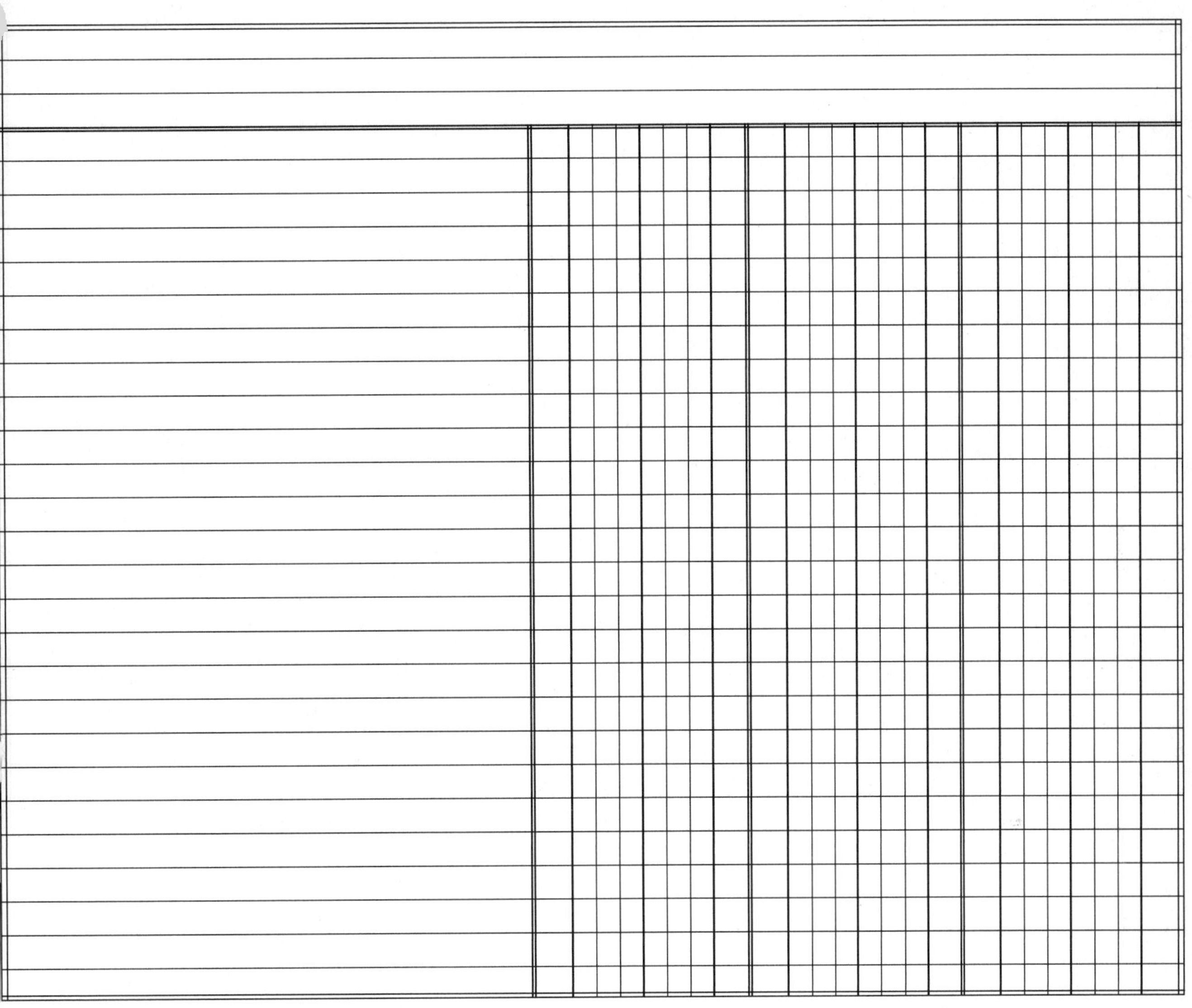

NAME
SECTION
DATE

Requirement 2

P5-6A
(Continued)

NAME
SECTION
DATE

P5-7A

Requirement 1

NAME
SECTION
DATE

Requirement 2

P5-7A
(Continued)

NAME
SECTION
DATE

P5-8A

Requirement 1

Requirement 2

NAME
SECTION
DATE

P5-9A

Requirement 1

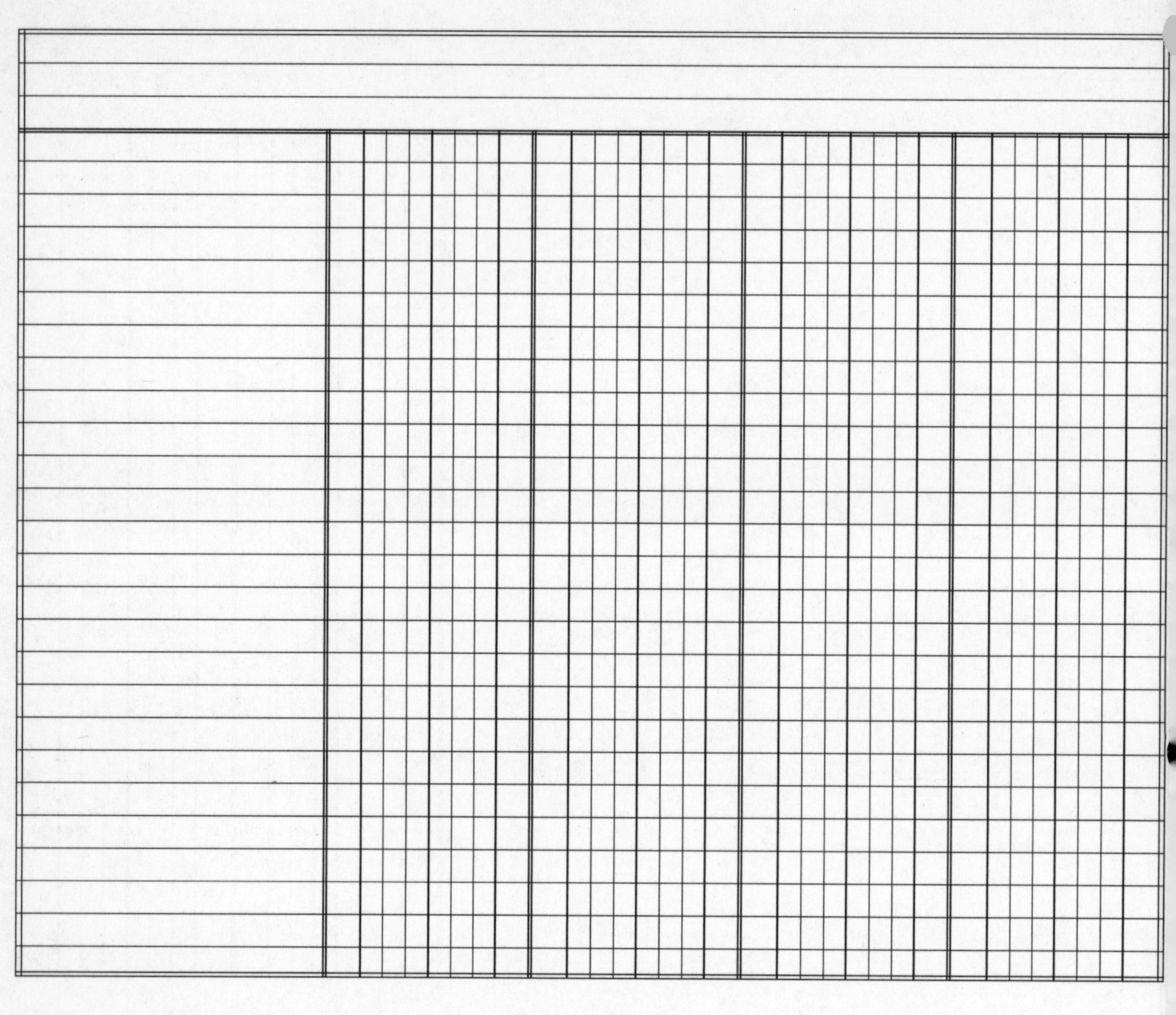

Requirements 2 & 3

NAME
SECTION
DATE

P5-10A

Requirement 1

Journal

DATE		ACCOUNT TITLES AND EXPLANATION	POST REF.	DEBIT	CREDIT

NAME
SECTION
DATE

Requirement 1 (Continued)

P5-10A
(Continued)

Journal				
DATE	ACCOUNT TITLES AND EXPLANATION	POST REF.	DEBIT	CREDIT

Requirement 2

NAME
SECTION
DATE

P5-10A
(Continued)

Requirement 3

Requirement 4

NAME
SECTION
DATE

P5-11A

Requirement 1

Journal				
DATE	ACCOUNT TITLES AND EXPLANATION	POST REF.	DEBIT	CREDIT

NAME
SECTION
DATE

P5-11A
(Continued)

Requirement 2

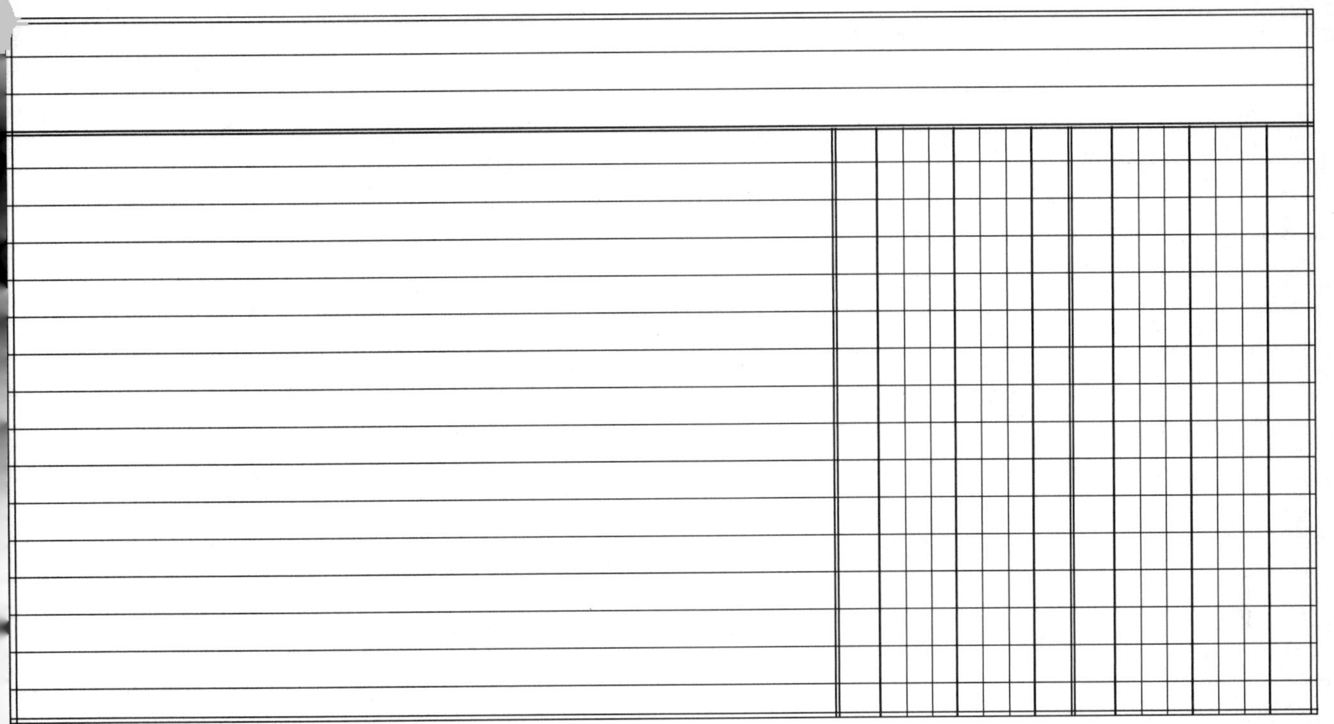

NAME
SECTION
DATE

P5-11A
(Continued)

Requirement 2 (Continued)

ME
CTION
TE

P5-1B

NAME
SECTION
DATE

P5-2B

Journal

DATE		ACCOUNT TITLES AND EXPLANATION	POST REF.	DEBIT	CREDIT

AME
ECTION
ATE

P5-3B

Requirement 1

Journal

DATE		ACCOUNT TITLES AND EXPLANATION	POST REF.	DEBIT	CREDIT

NAME
SECTION
DATE

Requirement 1 (Continued)

P5-3B
(Continued)

Journal

DATE		ACCOUNT TITLES AND EXPLANATION	POST REF.	DEBIT	CREDIT

Requirement 2

AME
ECTION
ATE

P5-4B

The foldout work sheet to solve this problem can be found in the back of the book.

P5-5B

Requirement 1

Journal

DATE	ACCOUNT TITLES AND EXPLANATION	POST REF.	DEBIT	CREDIT

NAME
SECTION
DATE

P5-5E
(Continue

Requirement 1 (Continued)

Journal

DATE		ACCOUNT TITLES AND EXPLANATION	POST REF.	DEBIT	CREDIT

Requirement 2

AME
ECTION
ATE

P5-6B

Requirement 1

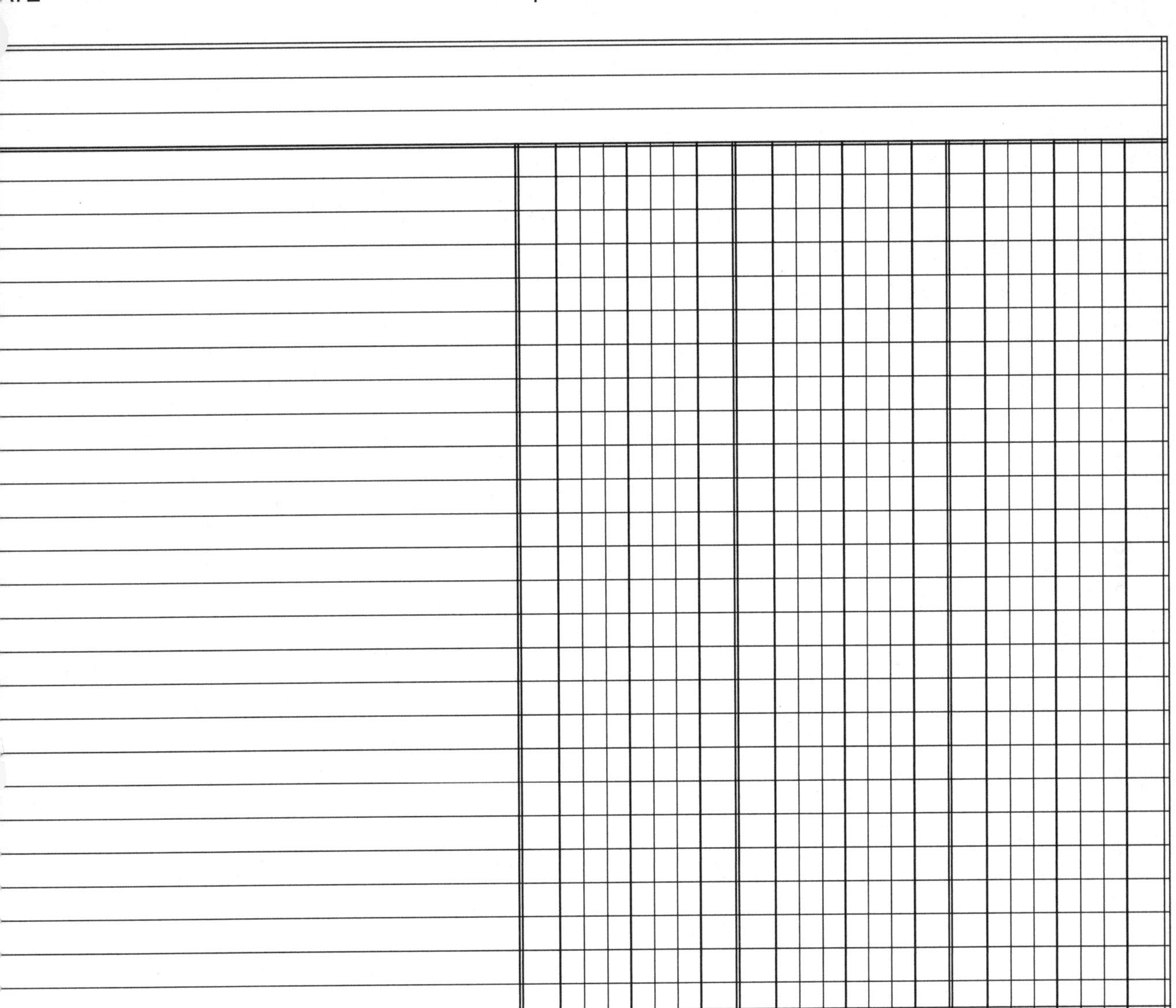

NAME
SECTION
DATE

Requirement 2

P5-6B
(Continue

AME
ECTION
ATE

P5-7B

Requirement 1

NAME
SECTION
DATE

Requirement 2

P5-7B

(Continued

AME
ECTION
ATE

P5-8B

Requirement 1

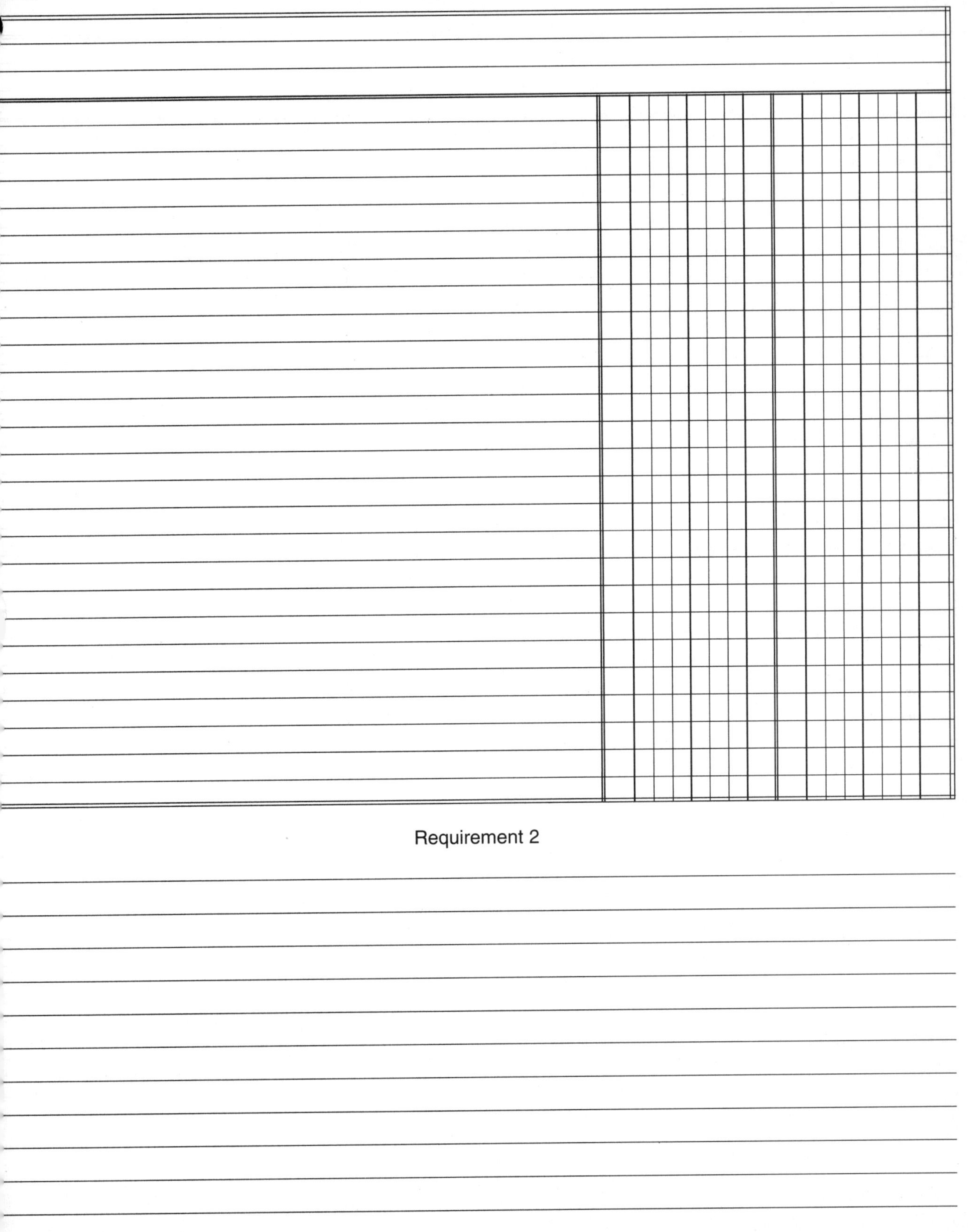

Requirement 2

NAME
SECTION
DATE

P5-9E

Requirement 1

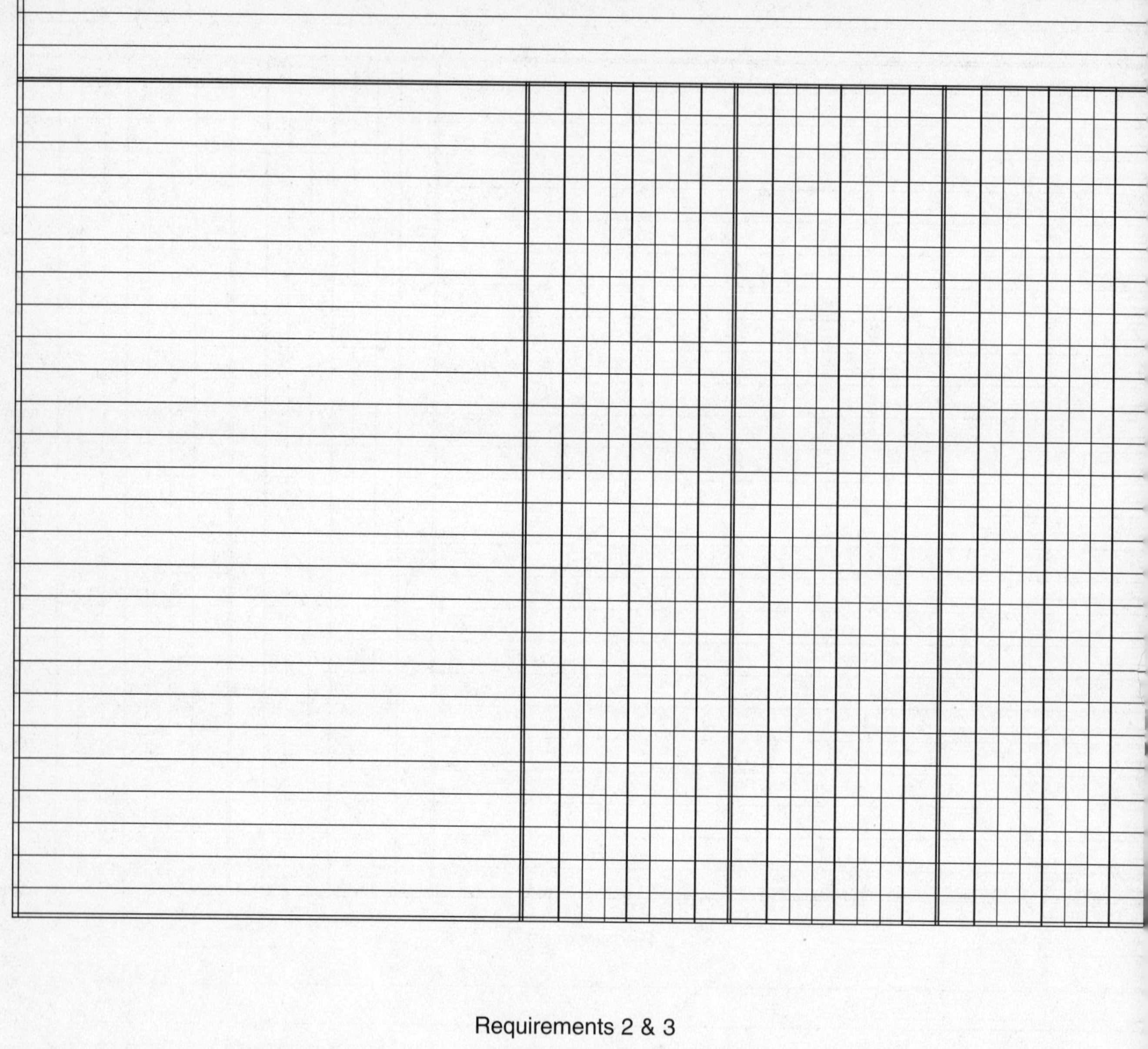

Requirements 2 & 3

AME
ECTION
ATE

P5-10B

Requirement 1

Journal

DATE		ACCOUNT TITLES AND EXPLANATION	POST REF.	DEBIT	CREDIT

NAME
SECTION
DATE

P5-10B
(Continued)

Requirement 1 (Continued)

Journal

DATE		ACCOUNT TITLES AND EXPLANATION	POST REF.	DEBIT	CREDIT

Requirement 2

NAME
SECTION
DATE

P5-10B
(Continued)

Requirement 3

Requirement 4

NAME
SECTION
DATE

P5-11B

Requirement 1

Journal

DATE		ACCOUNT TITLES AND EXPLANATION	POST REF.	DEBIT	CREDIT

NAME
SECTION
DATE

Requirement 2

P5-11B
(Continued)

NAME
SECTION
DATE

P5-11B
(Continued)

Requirement 2 (Continued)

NAME
SECTION
DATE

P5-1C

Requirement 1

NAME
SECTION
DATE

Requirement 2

P5-1C
(Continued)

AME
ECTION
ATE

P5-2C

NAME
SECTION
DATE

Decision Problem 1

Requirement 1

Gross Margin Percentage

Current Ratio

Debt Ratio

Inventory Turnover

NAME
SECTION
DATE

Decision Problem 1

(Continued)

Requirement 2

NAME
SECTION
DATE

Decision Problem 1

(Continued

Requirement 2 (Continued)

NAME
SECTION
DATE

Decision Problem 1

(Continued)

Requirement 3

Gross Margin Percentage

Current Ratio

Debt Ratio

Inventory Turnover

NAME
SECTION
DATE

Decision Problem 1

(Continued)

Requirement 4

NAME
SECTION
DATE

Decision Problem 2

Requirements 1 & 2

NAME
SECTION
DATE

Decision Problem 3

Requirements 1 & 2

NAME
SECTION
DATE

Financial Statement Problem

Requirement 1

Journal

DATE		ACCOUNT TITLES AND EXPLANATION	POST REF.	DEBIT	CREDIT

Requirements 2 & 3

NAME
SECTION
DATE

E5S-1

Journal

DATE		ACCOUNT TITLES AND EXPLANATION	POST REF.	DEBIT	CREDIT

NAME
SECTION
DATE

Requirements 1 – 3

E5S-2

Journal

DATE		ACCOUNT TITLES AND EXPLANATION	POST REF.	DEBIT	CREDIT

E5S-3

Journal

DATE		ACCOUNT TITLES AND EXPLANATION	POST REF.	DEBIT	CREDIT

NAME
SECTION
DATE

E5S-4

Journal

DATE		ACCOUNT TITLES AND EXPLANATION	POST REF.	DEBIT	CREDIT

NAME
SECTION
DATE

P5S-1

Journal

DATE		ACCOUNT TITLES AND EXPLANATION	POST REF.	DEBIT	CREDIT

NAME
SECTION
DATE

P5S-1

(Continued)

Journal

DATE		ACCOUNT TITLES AND EXPLANATION	POST REF.	DEBIT	CREDIT

NAME
SECTION
DATE

P5S-2

Requirement 1

Journal

DATE		ACCOUNT TITLES AND EXPLANATION	POST REF.	DEBIT	CREDIT

NAME
SECTION
DATE

P5S-2
(Continued)

Requirement 1 (Continued)

Journal

DATE		ACCOUNT TITLES AND EXPLANATION	POST REF.	DEBIT	CREDIT

Requirement 2

NAME
SECTION
DATE

P5S-3

Requirement 1

Journal

DATE		ACCOUNT TITLES AND EXPLANATION	POST REF.	DEBIT	CREDIT

NAME
SECTION
DATE

Requirement 1 (Continued)

P5S-3
(Continued)

Journal

DATE		ACCOUNT TITLES AND EXPLANATION	POST REF.	DEBIT	CREDIT

Requirement 2

NAME
SECTION
DATE

P5S-4

Requirement 1

The foldout work sheet to solve this problem can be found in the back of the book.

Requirement 2

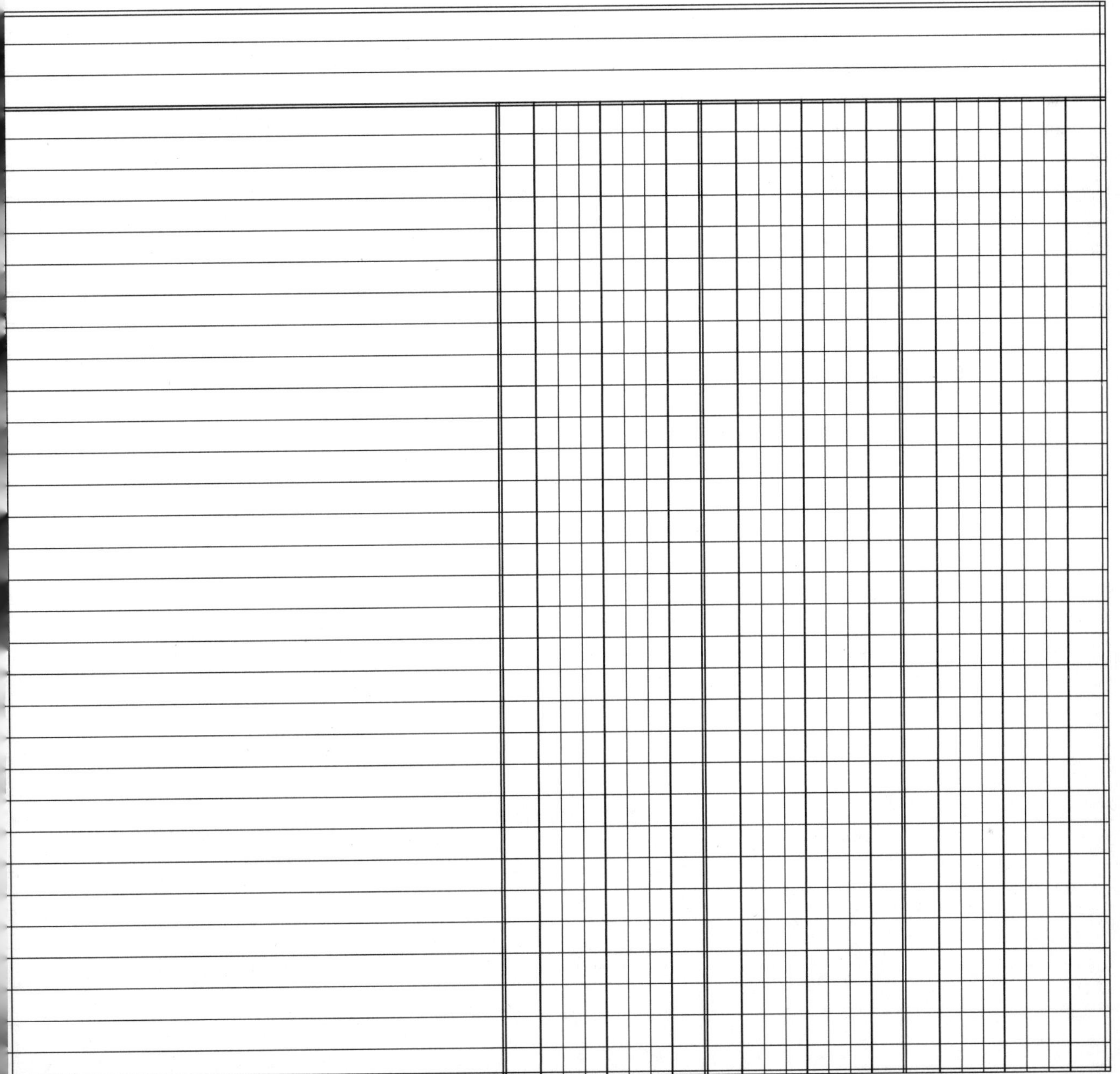

NAME
SECTION
DATE

P5S-4

Requirement 2 (Continued)

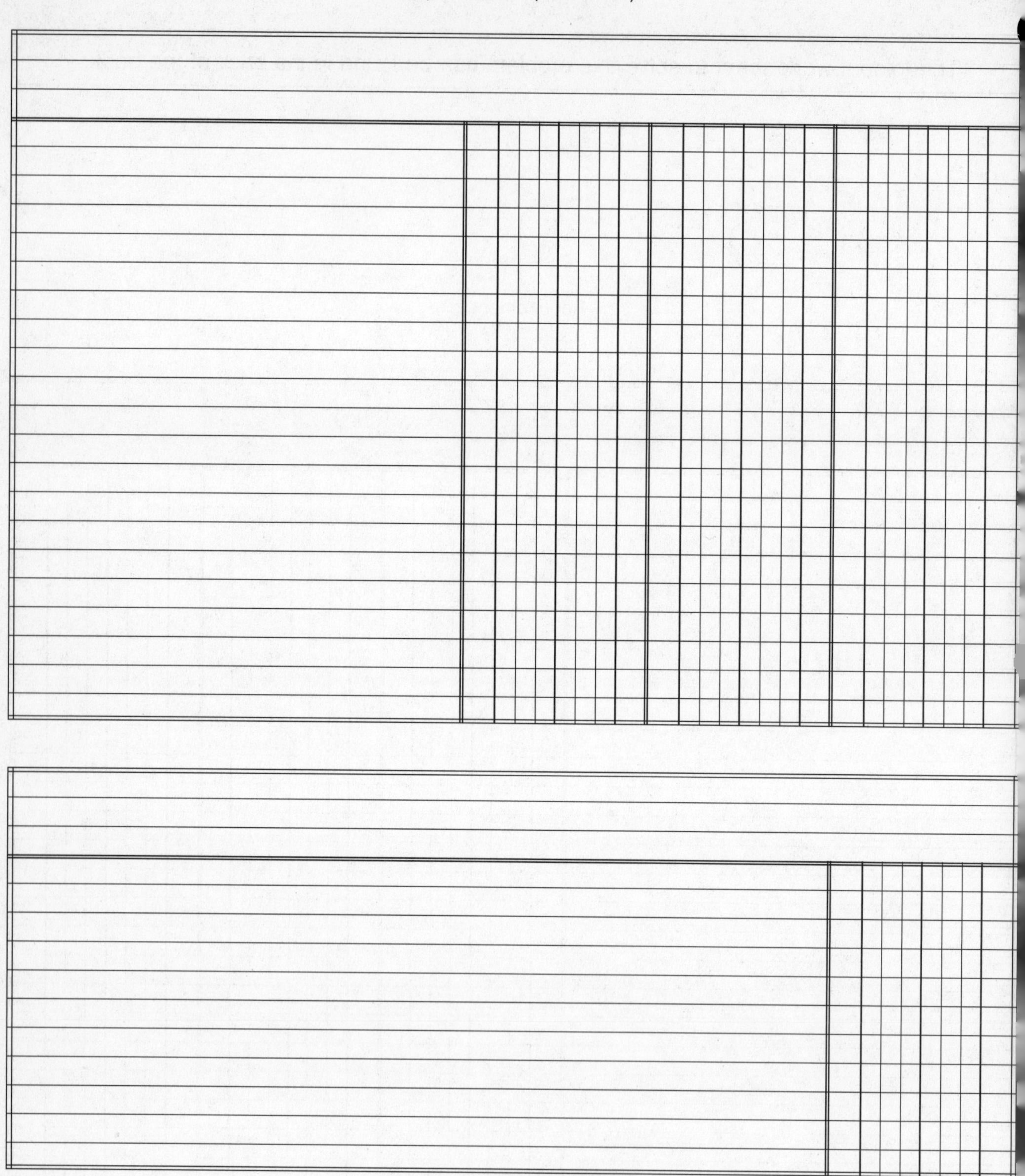

NAME
SECTION
DATE

P5S-4
(Continued)

Requirement 2 (Continued)

NAME
SECTION
DATE

Requirement 3

P5S-4
(Continued

Journal

DATE		ACCOUNT TITLES AND EXPLANATION	POST REF.	DEBIT	CREDIT

AME
ECTION
ATE

Requirement 3 (Continued)

P5S-4

(Continued)

Journal

DATE		ACCOUNT TITLES AND EXPLANATION	POST REF.	DEBIT	CREDIT

NAME
SECTION
DATE

Requirement 4

P5S-4
(Continued)

NAME
SECTION
DATE

Chapter 6

E6-1

Perpetual Inventory Record

ITEM:

DATE	RECEIVED QTY.	RECEIVED UNIT COST	RECEIVED TOTAL COST	SOLD QTY.	SOLD UNIT COST	SOLD TOTAL COST	BALANCE QTY.	BALANCE UNIT COST	BALANCE TOTAL COST

COMPUTATIONS:

NAME
SECTION
DATE

E6-2

Requirement

Journal

DATE		DESCRIPTION	POST REF.	DEBIT	CREDIT

NAME
SECTION
DATE

E6-3

Perpetual Inventory Record

ITEM:

DATE		RECEIVED			SOLD			BALANCE		
		QTY.	UNIT COST	TOTAL COST	QTY.	UNIT COST	TOTAL COST	QTY.	UNIT COST	TOTAL COST

COMPUTATIONS:

NAME
SECTION
DATE

E6-4

Perpetual Inventory Record

ITEM:

DATE		RECEIVED			SOLD			BALANCE		
		QTY.	UNIT COST	TOTAL COST	QTY.	UNIT COST	TOTAL COST	QTY.	UNIT COST	TOTAL COST

COMPUTATIONS:

NAME
SECTION
DATE

E6-5

Requirement 1

Journal

DATE		ACCOUNT TITLES AND EXPLANATION	POST REF.	DEBIT	CREDIT

NAME
SECTION
DATE

Requirement 2

E6-5
(Continued)

COMPUTATIONS:

NAME
SECTION
DATE

E6-6

ACCOUNTS	DEBIT/CREDIT AMOUNTS					
	WEIGHTED-AVERAGE		FIFO		LIFO	

COMPUTATIONS:

NAME
SECTION
DATE

E6-7

Requirements 1 – 4

	ENDING INVENTORY	COST OF GOODS SOLD
1. SPECIFIC UNIT COST:		
2. WEIGHTED-AVERAGE COST:		
3. FIFO:		
4. LIFO:		

NAME
SECTION
DATE

Part 1

E6-8

NAME
SECTION
DATE

E6-8
(Continued)

Part 2

NAME
SECTION
DATE

E6-9

a. ____________________

b. ____________________

c. ____________________

d. ____________________

e. ____________________

f. ____________________

g. ____________________

h. ____________________

E6-10

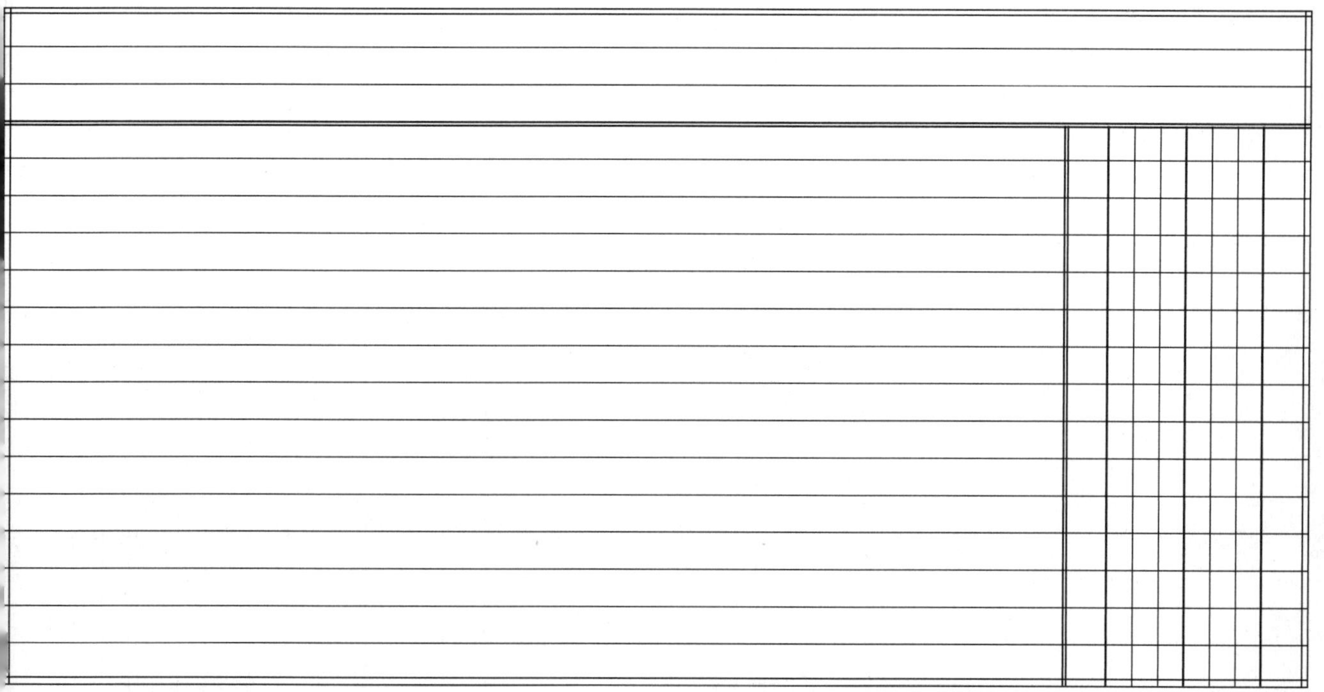

NAME
SECTION
DATE

E6-11

NAME
SECTION
DATE

E6-12

	2005	2004

NAME
SECTION
DATE

E6-13

Requirements 1 – 3

NAME
SECTION
DATE

E6-14

Requirements 1 – 5

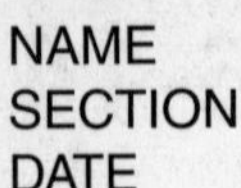

E6-15

NAME
SECTION
DATE

E6-16

	TEENAGE LINE		YOUNG WOMAN LINE		MATURE LINE	

NAME
SECTION
DATE

E6-17

a. – f.

E6-18

NAME
SECTION
DATE

Beyond the Numbers 6-1

Requirements 1 – 3

NAME
SECTION
DATE

Beyond the Numbers 6-1

(Continued)

Requirements 1 – 3 (Continued)

NAME
SECTION
DATE

Ethical Issue

Requirements 1 – 3

NAME
SECTION
DATE

P6-1A

Requirement 1

Perpetual Inventory Record

ITEM:

DATE		RECEIVED			SOLD			BALANCE		
		QTY.	UNIT COST	TOTAL COST	QTY.	UNIT COST	TOTAL COST	QTY.	UNIT COST	TOTAL COST

COMPUTATIONS:

NAME
SECTION
DATE

Requirement 2

P6-1A
(Continued)

Journal

DATE		DESCRIPTION	POST REF.	DEBIT	CREDIT

NAME
SECTION
DATE

P6-2A

Requirement 1

Perpetual Inventory Record

ITEM:

DATE		RECEIVED			SOLD			BALANCE		
		QTY.	UNIT COST	TOTAL COST	QTY.	UNIT COST	TOTAL COST	QTY.	UNIT COST	TOTAL COST

Requirement 2

NAME
SECTION
DATE

P6-3A

Requirement 1

Perpetual Inventory Record

ITEM:

DATE	RECEIVED			SOLD			BALANCE		
	QTY.	UNIT COST	TOTAL COST	QTY.	UNIT COST	TOTAL COST	QTY.	UNIT COST	TOTAL COST

Requirement 2

Requirement 3

NAME
SECTION
DATE

P6-4A

Journal

DATE	DESCRIPTION	POST REF.	DEBIT	CREDIT

NAME
SECTION
DATE

P6-4A
(Continued)

Requirement 2

Requirement 3

NAME
SECTION
DATE

P6-5A

Requirement 1

	ENDING INVENTORY	COST OF GOODS SOLD
1. WEIGHTED-AVERAGE COST:		
2. FIFO:		
3. LIFO:		

NAME
SECTION
DATE

P6-5A
(Continued)

Requirement 2

ACCOUNT	FIFO	WEIGHTED AVERAGE	LIFO

Requirement 3

NAME
SECTION
DATE

P6-6A

Requirements 1 & 2

NAME
SECTION
DATE

P6-7A

Requirement 1

Requirement 2

PERPETUAL SYSTEM		PERIODIC SYSTEM	

Requirement 3

NAME
SECTION
DATE

P6-8A

NAME
SECTION
DATE

P6-9A

Requirement 1

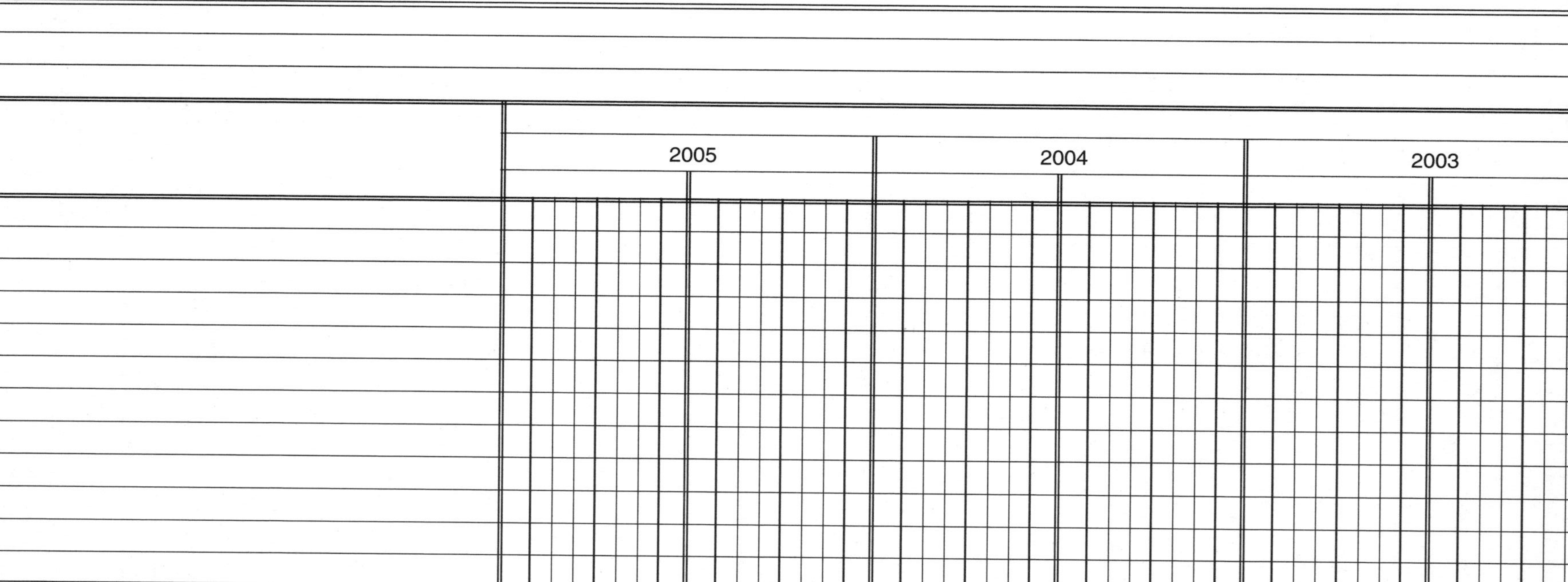

	2005	2004	2003

Requirement 2

NAME
SECTION
DATE

P6-10A

Requirement 1

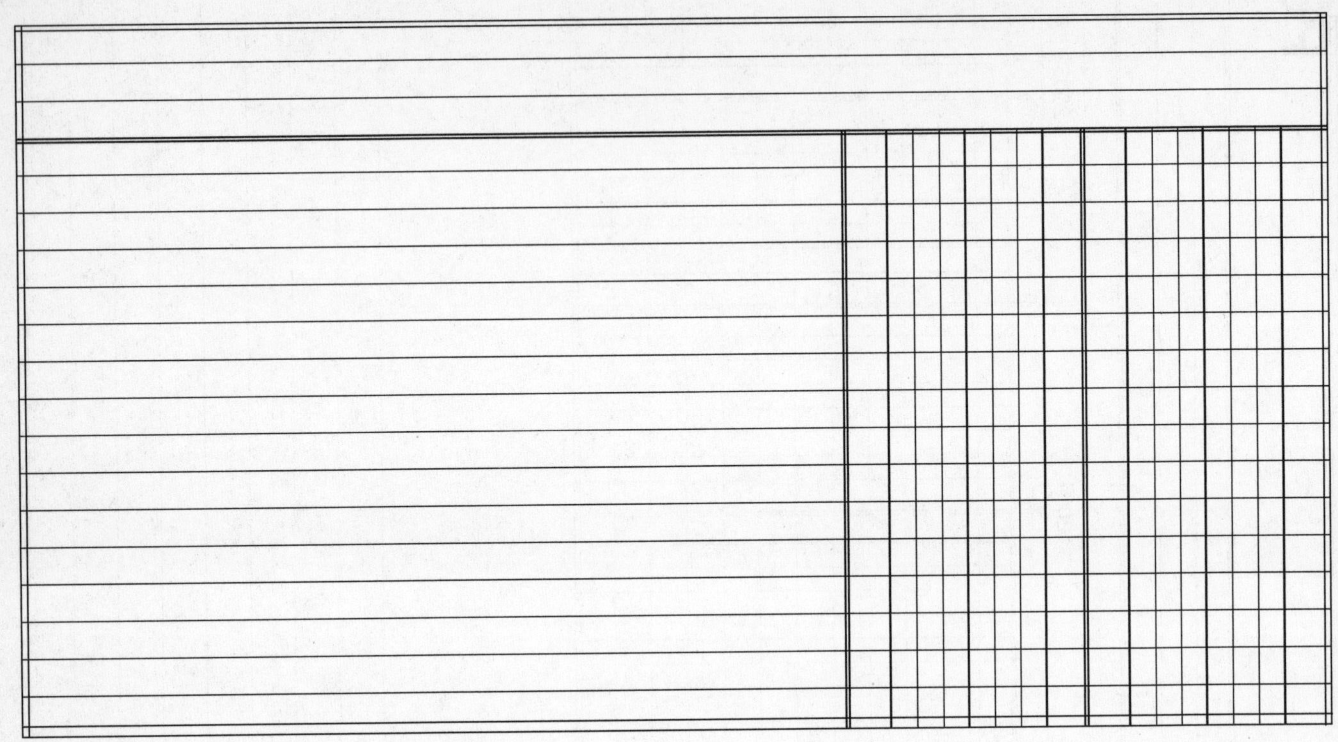

Requirement 2

NAME
SECTION
DATE

P6-11A

Requirement 1

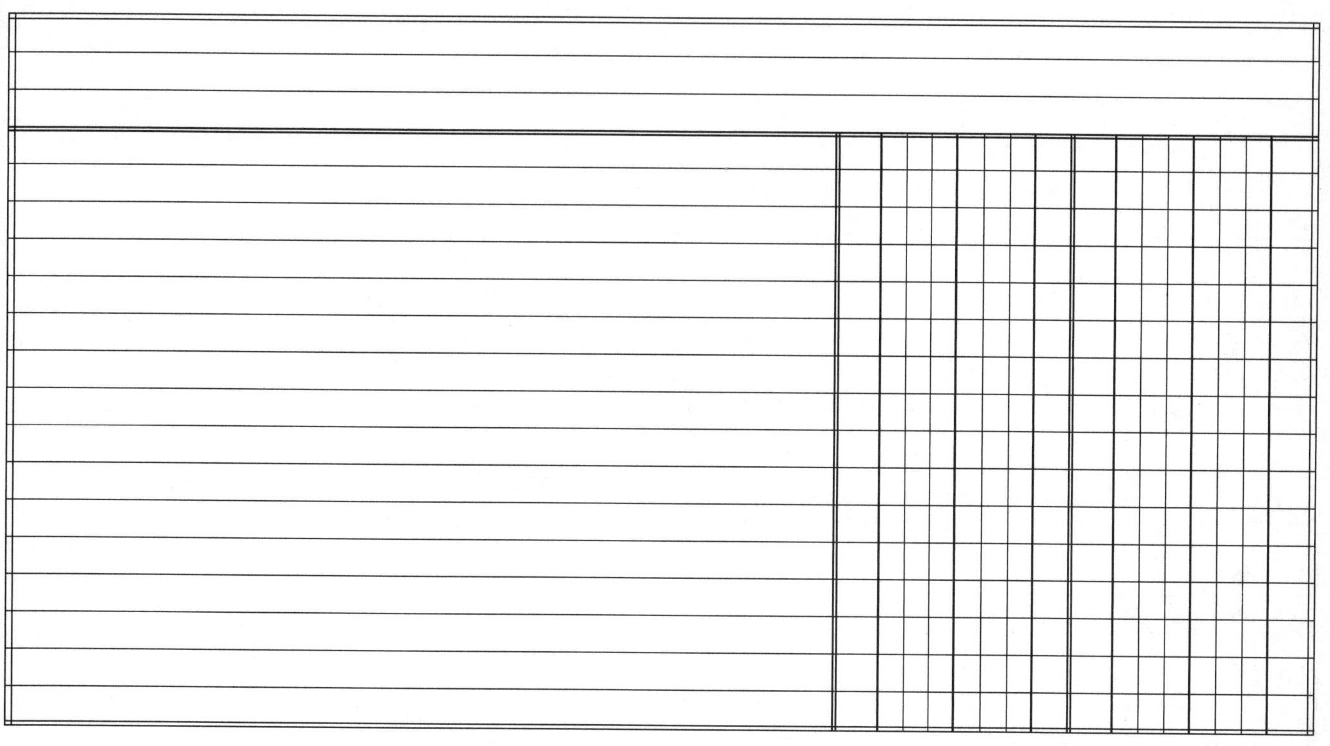

Requirement 2

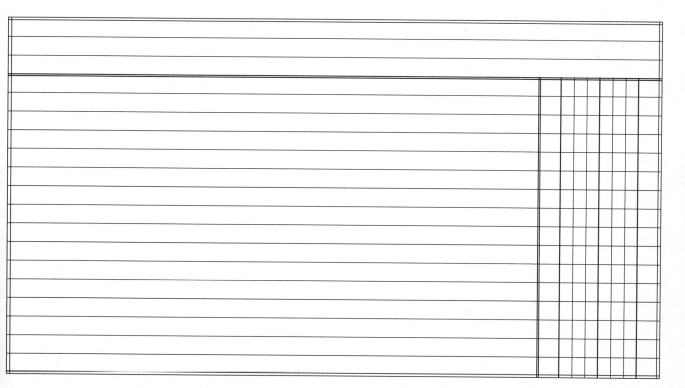

NAME
SECTION
DATE

P6-11A
(Continued)

Requirement 3

Requirement 4

Journal				
DATE	ACCOUNT TITLES AND EXPLANATION	POST REF.	DEBIT	CREDIT

Requirement 5

NAME
SECTION
DATE

P6-12A

Requirement 1

Perpetual Inventory Record

ITEM:

DATE		RECEIVED			SOLD			BALANCE		
		QTY.	UNIT COST	TOTAL COST	QTY.	UNIT COST	TOTAL COST	QTY.	UNIT COST	TOTAL COST

Perpetual Inventory Record

ITEM:

DATE		RECEIVED			SOLD			BALANCE		
		QTY.	UNIT COST	TOTAL COST	QTY.	UNIT COST	TOTAL COST	QTY.	UNIT COST	TOTAL COST

NAME
SECTION
DATE

P6-12A
(Continued)

Requirement 2

Journal

DATE		ACCOUNT TITLES AND EXPLANATION	POST REF.	DEBIT	CREDIT

Requirement 3

NAME
SECTION
DATE

P6-12A
(Continued)

Requirement 3 (Continued)

Journal

DATE		ACCOUNT TITLES AND EXPLANATION	POST REF.	DEBIT	CREDIT

Requirement 4

NAME
SECTION
DATE

P6-1B

Requirement 1

Perpetual Inventory Record

ITEM:

DATE	RECEIVED			SOLD			BALANCE		
	QTY.	UNIT COST	TOTAL COST	QTY.	UNIT COST	TOTAL COST	QTY.	UNIT COST	TOTAL COST

COMPUTATIONS:

NAME
SECTION
DATE

Requirement 2

P6-1B
(Continued)

Journal

DATE		DESCRIPTION	POST REF.	DEBIT	CREDIT

NAME
SECTION
DATE

P6-2B

Requirement 1

Perpetual Inventory Record

ITEM:

DATE		RECEIVED			SOLD			BALANCE		
		QTY.	UNIT COST	TOTAL COST	QTY.	UNIT COST	TOTAL COST	QTY.	UNIT COST	TOTAL COST

Requirement 2

NAME
SECTION
DATE

P6-3B

Requirement 1

Perpetual Inventory Record

ITEM:

DATE	RECEIVED			SOLD			BALANCE		
	QTY.	UNIT COST	TOTAL COST	QTY.	UNIT COST	TOTAL COST	QTY.	UNIT COST	TOTAL COST

Requirement 2

Requirement 3

NAME
SECTION
DATE

P6-4B

Journal

DATE		DESCRIPTION	POST REF.	DEBIT	CREDIT

NAME
SECTION
DATE

P6-4B
(Continued)

Requirement 2

Requirement 3

NAME
SECTION
DATE

P6-5B

Requirement 1

	ENDING INVENTORY	COST OF GOODS SOLD
1. WEIGHTED-AVERAGE COST:		
2. FIFO:		
3. LIFO:		

NAME
SECTION
DATE

P6-5B
(Continued)

Requirement 2

ACCOUNT	FIFO	WEIGHTED AVERAGE	LIFO

Requirements 3 & 4

NAME
SECTION
DATE

P6-6B

Requirements 1 & 2

NAME
SECTION
DATE

P6-7B

Requirement 1

Requirement 2

PERPETUAL SYSTEM			PERIODIC SYSTEM		

Requirement 3

NAME
SECTION
DATE

P6-8B

NAME
SECTION
DATE

P6-9B

Requirement 1

	2005		2004		2003	

Requirement 2

NAME
SECTION
DATE

P6-10B

Requirement 1

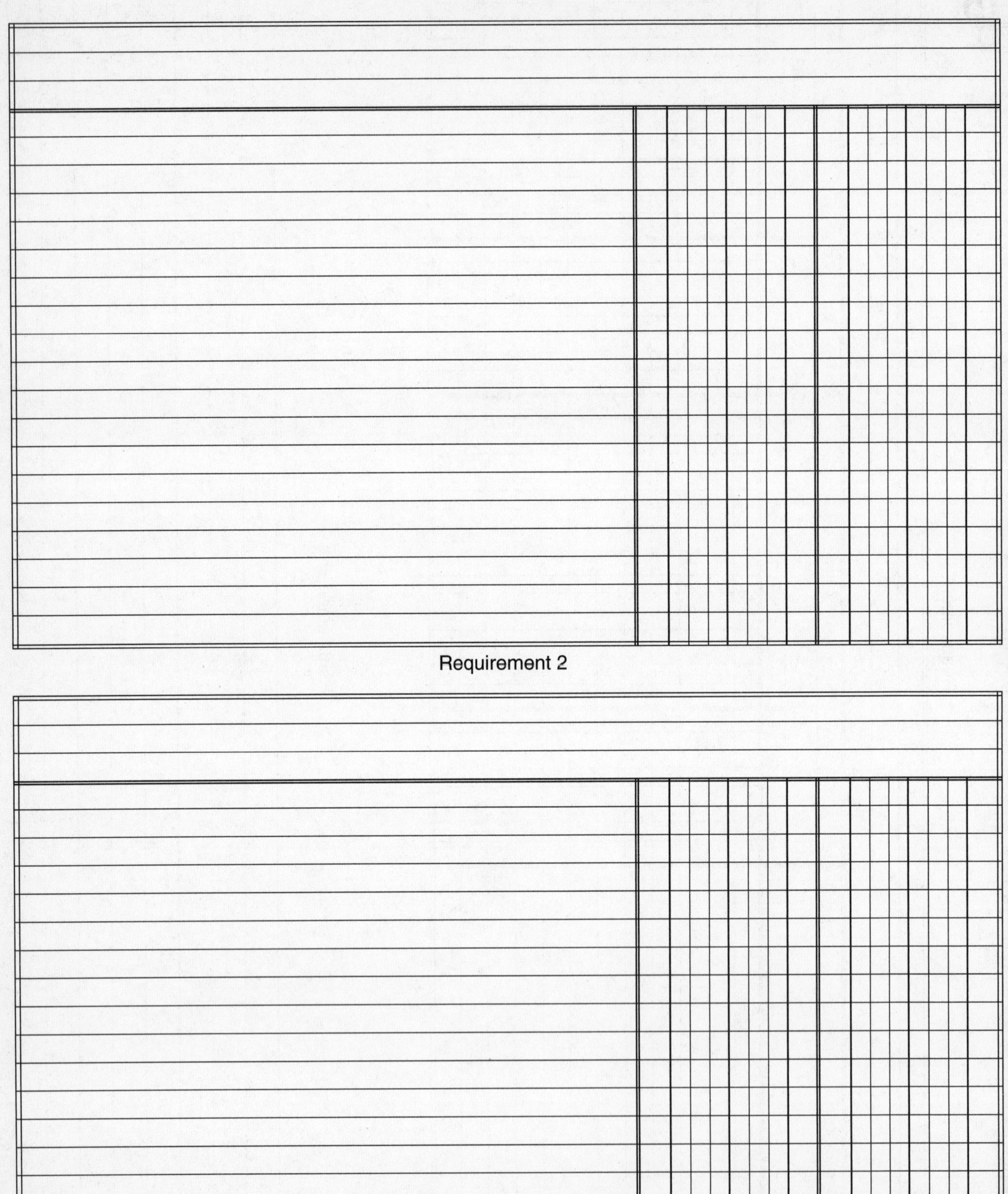

Requirement 2

AME
ECTION
ATE

P6-11B

Requirement 1

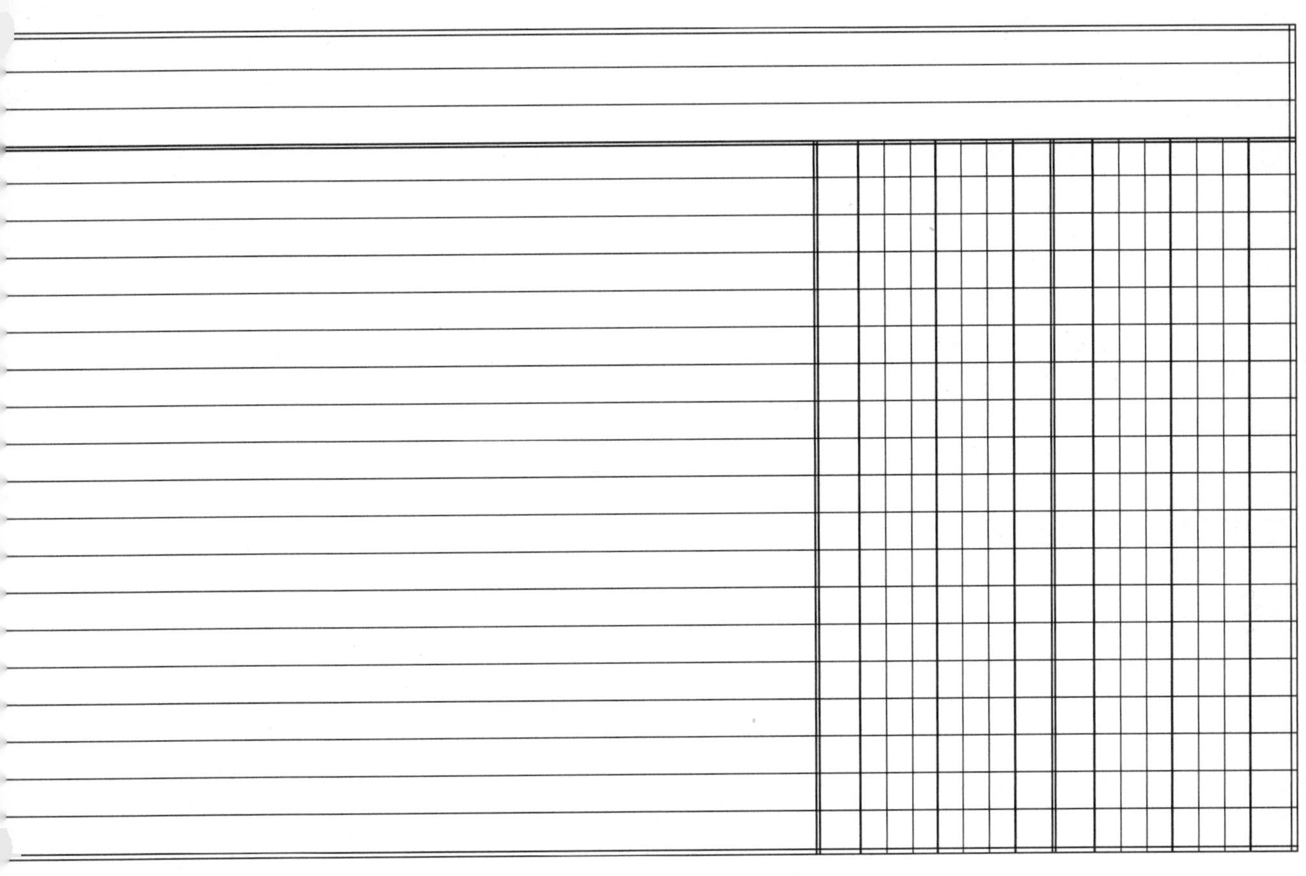

Requirement 2

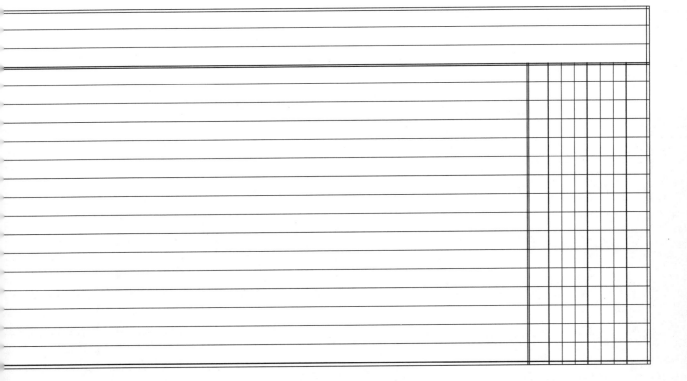

NAME
SECTION
DATE

P6-11E
(Continue

Requirement 3

Requirement 4

Journal

DATE		ACCOUNT TITLES AND EXPLANATION	POST REF.	DEBIT	CREDIT

NAME
SECTION
DATE

Requirement 1

P6-12B

Perpetual Inventory Record

ITEM:

DATE		RECEIVED			SOLD			BALANCE		
		QTY.	UNIT COST	TOTAL COST	QTY.	UNIT COST	TOTAL COST	QTY.	UNIT COST	TOTAL COST

Perpetual Inventory Record

ITEM:

DATE		RECEIVED			SOLD			BALANCE		
		QTY.	UNIT COST	TOTAL COST	QTY.	UNIT COST	TOTAL COST	QTY.	UNIT COST	TOTAL COST

NAME
SECTION
DATE

P6-12B
(Continued)

Requirement 2

Journal

DATE	ACCOUNT TITLES AND EXPLANATION	POST REF.	DEBIT	CREDIT

Requirement 3

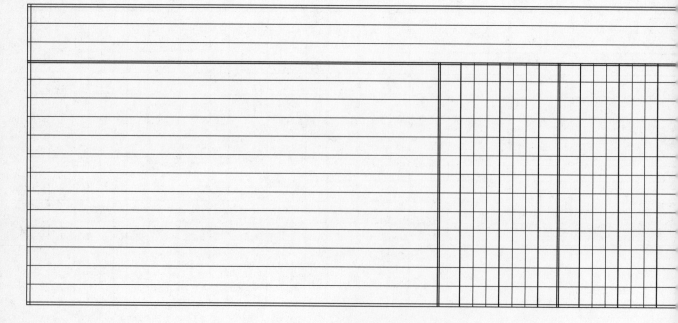

AME
ECTION
ATE

P6-12B
(Continued)

Requirement 3 (Continued)

Journal

DATE		ACCOUNT TITLES AND EXPLANATION	POST REF.	DEBIT	CREDIT

Requirement 4

NAME
SECTION
DATE

P6-1C

AME
ECTION
ATE

P6-2C

NAME
SECTION
DATE

Decision Problem

Requirements 1 & 2

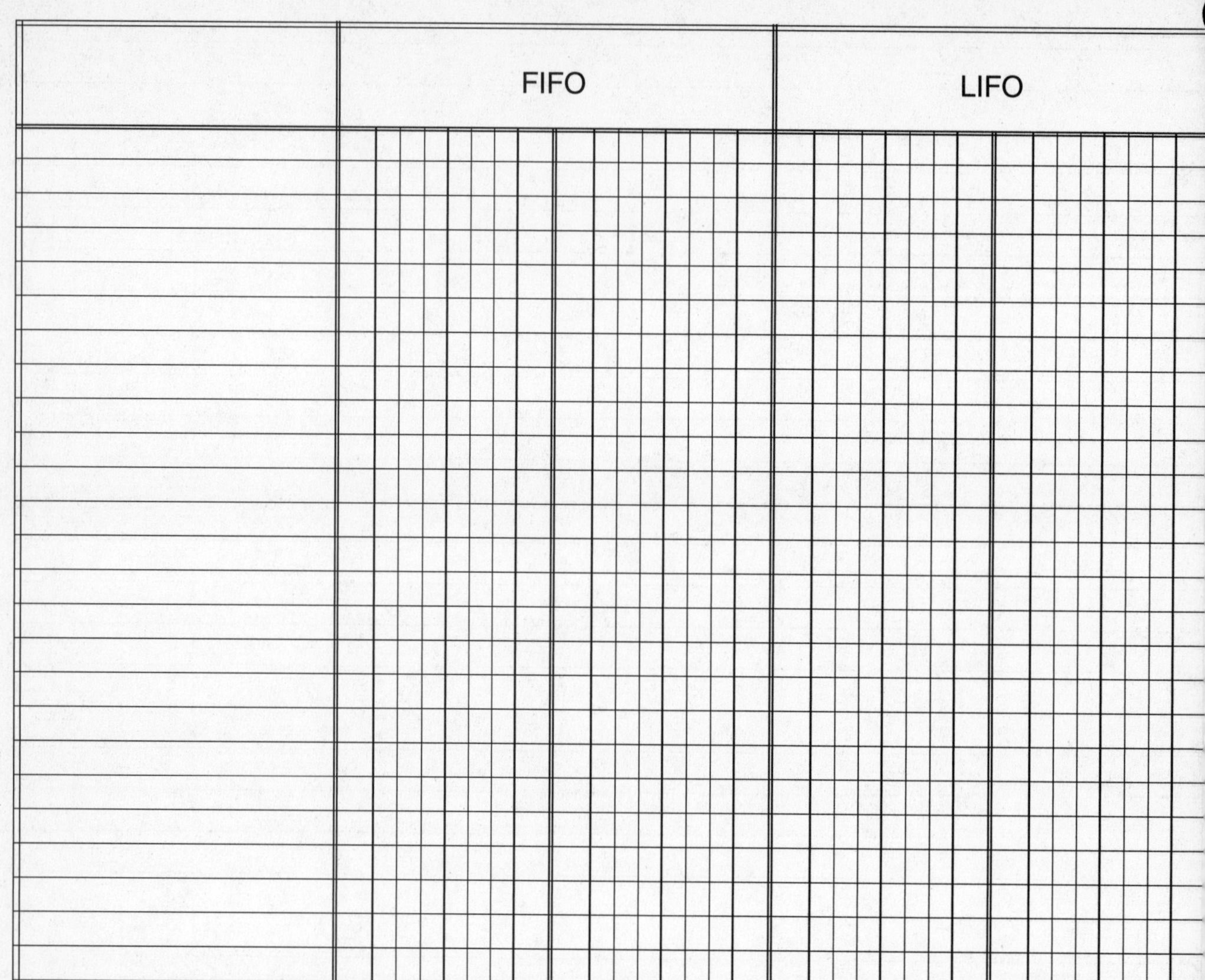

NAME
SECTION
DATE

Decision Problem

(Continued)

Requirements 1 & 2

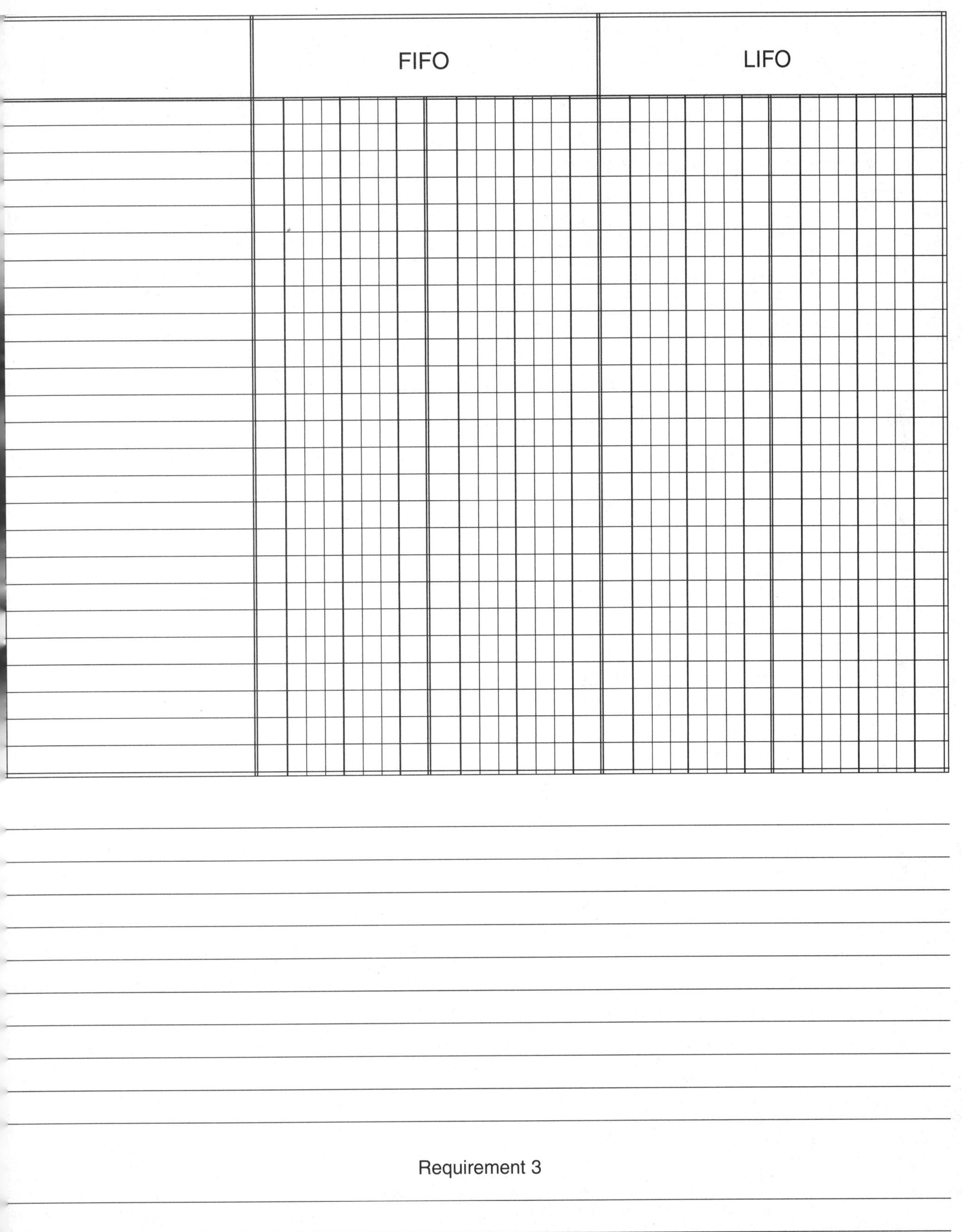

	FIFO	LIFO

Requirement 3

NAME
SECTION
DATE

Financial Statement Problem

Requirements 1 – 4

AME
ECTION
ATE

Chapter 7

E7-1

E7-2

NAME
SECTION
DATE

E7-3

E7-4

E7-5

AME
ECTION
ATE

E7-6

E7-7

a. – c.

NAME
SECTION
DATE

E7-8

Cash Receipts Journal

	Debits		Credits					PAGE
					Other Accounts			
DATE	CASH	SALES DISCOUNTS	ACCOUNTS RECEIVABLE	SALES REVENUE	ACCOUNT TITLE	POST REF.	AMOUNT	COST OF GOODS SOLD Dr. INVENTORY Cr.

NAME
SECTION
DATE

E7-9

POSTING REFERENCE	ACTUAL REFERENCE	POSTING REFERENCE	ACTUAL REFERENCE
a		f	
b		g	
c		h	
d		i	
e		j	

E7-10

NAME
SECTION
DATE

E7-11

General Journal

DATE		ACCOUNT TITLES AND EXPLANATION	POST REF.	DEBIT	CREDIT

NAME
SECTION
DATE

E7-11
(Continued)

Purchases Journal

PAGE

DATE	ACCOUNT CREDITED	TERMS	POST REF.	CREDITS	DEBITS		OTHER ACCOUNTS		
				ACCOUNTS PAYABLE	INVENTORY	SUPPLIES	ACCOUNT TITLE	POST. REF.	AMOUNT

NAME
SECTION
DATE

E7-12

Requirement 1

Account:						Account No.
Date		Item	Jrnl. Ref.	Debit	Credit	Balance

Account:						Account No.
Date		Item	Jrnl. Ref.	Debit	Credit	Balance

Account:						Account No.
Date		Item	Jrnl. Ref.	Debit	Credit	Balance

Account:						Account No.
Date		Item	Jrnl. Ref.	Debit	Credit	Balance

AME
ECTION
ATE

E7-12
(Continued)

Requirement 2

Account:						Account No.
Date		Item	Jrnl. Ref.	Debit	Credit	Balance

Account:						Account No.
Date		Item	Jrnl. Ref.	Debit	Credit	Balance

Account:						Account No.
Date		Item	Jrnl. Ref.	Debit	Credit	Balance

Requirements 3 & 4

NAME
SECTION
DATE

E7-13

Requirements 1 – 3

Cash Payments Journal

PAGE

					Debits		Credits	
DATE	CHQ. NO.	PAYEE	ACCOUNT DEBITED	POST REF.	OTHER ACCOUNTS	ACCOUNTS PAYABLE	INVENTORY	CASH

NAME
SECTION
DATE

E7-14

EDDIE'S BICYCLE SHOP JOURNAL ENTRIES

SCHWINN JOURNAL ENTRIES

General Journal

DATE	ACCOUNT TITLE	DEBIT	CREDIT	DATE	ACCOUNT TITLE	DEBIT	CREDIT

NAME
SECTION
DATE

E7-15

Requirement 1

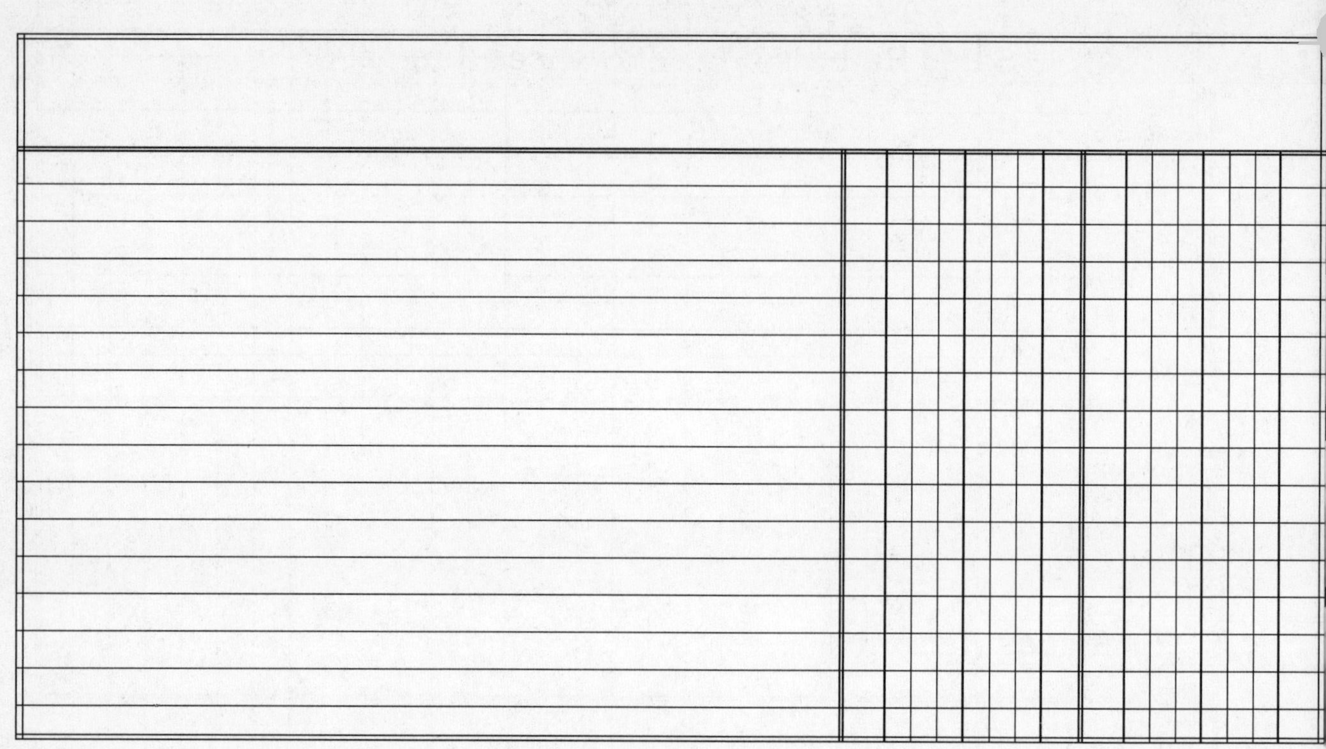

Requirement 2

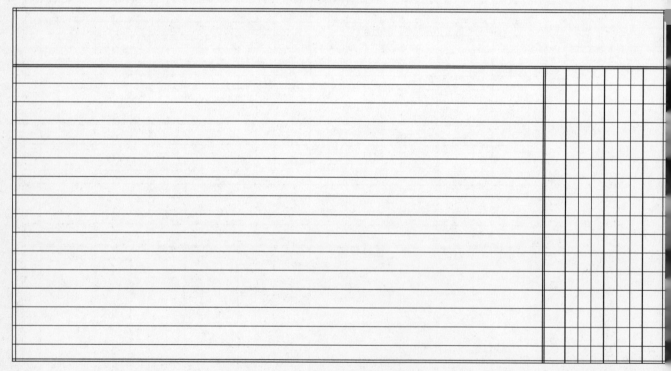

AME
ECTION
ATE

Beyond the Numbers 7-1

Sales Returns and Allowances Journal					
Date	Credit Memo No.	Account Credited	Post. Ref.	Sales Returns and Allowances Dr. Accounts Receivable Cr.	Inventory Dr. Cost of Goods Sold Cr.

Purchases Returns and Allowances Journal				
Date	Debit Memo No.	Account Credited	Post. Ref.	Accounts Payable Dr. Inventory Cr.

NAME
SECTION
DATE

Ethical Issue

Requirements 1 – 3

NAME
SECTION
DATE

P7-1A

Requirements 1 & 2

Row Number	Column A	B
5	Assets:	
6	Current assets:	
7	Cash ⟶	
8	Receivables ⟶	
9	Inventory ⟶	
10		______
11	Total current assets	
12		______
13	Equipment ⟶	
14	Accumulated amortization ⟶	
15		______
16	Equipment, net ⟶	
17		______
18	Total assets ⟶	
19		======

NAME
SECTION
DATE

Requirement 3

P7-1A
(Continued)

NAME
SECTION
DATE

P7-2A

Requirement 1 – 3

Sales Journal

Date	Invoice No.	Account Debited	Post. Ref.	Accounts Receivable Dr. Sales Revenue Cr.	Cost of Goods Sold Dr. Inventory Cr.

NAME
SECTION
DATE

P7-2A
(Continued)

Requirement 1 – 3 (Continued)

Cash Receipts Journal

PAGE

DATE	DEBITS		CREDITS					COST OF GOODS SOLD Dr. INVENTORY Cr.
					OTHER ACCOUNTS			
	CASH	SALES DISCOUNTS	ACCOUNTS RECEIVABLE	SALES REVENUE	ACCOUNT TITLE	POST REF.	AMOUNT	

NAME
SECTION
DATE

Requirements 1 – 3 (Continued)

P7-2A
(Continued)

General Journal

DATE		ACCOUNT TITLES AND EXPLANATION	POST REF.	DEBIT	CREDIT

NAME
SECTION
DATE

P7-3A

Requirement 1

Requirement 2

NAME
SECTION
DATE

Requirement 3

P7-3A
(Continued)

Cash Receipts Journal

DATE	DEBITS		CREDITS					PAGE
					OTHER ACCOUNTS			COST OF GOODS SOLD Dr. INVENTORY Cr.
	CASH	SALES DISCOUNTS	ACCOUNTS RECEIVABLE	SALES REVENUE	ACCOUNT TITLE	POST REF.	AMOUNT	

NAME
SECTION
DATE

P7-4A

Requirements 1 – 3

Purchases Journal

PAGE

				CREDITS	DEBITS				
							OTHER ACCOUNTS		
DATE	ACCOUNT CREDITED	TERMS	POST REF.	ACCOUNTS PAYABLE	INVENTORY	SUPPLIES	ACCOUNT TITLE	POST. REF.	AMOUNT

NAME
SECTION
DATE

Requirements 1 – 3 (Continued)

P7-4A
(Continued)

Cash Payments Journal

PAGE

					DEBITS		CREDITS	
DATE	CHQ. NO.	PAYEE	ACCOUNT DEBITED	POST REF.	OTHER ACCOUNTS	ACCOUNTS PAYABLE	INVENTORY	CASH

NAME
SECTION
DATE

Requirements 1 – 3 (Continued)

P7-4A
(Continued)

General Journal

DATE	ACCOUNT TITLES AND EXPLANATION	POST REF.	DEBIT	CREDIT

NAME
SECTION
DATE

P7-5A

Requirement 1

June 1

June 3

June 6

June 7

June 9

June 11

June 13

June 14

June 15

June 16

June 17

June 22

June 24

June 25

June 26

June 28

June 30

NAME
SECTION
DATE

Requirements 2 & 3

P7-5A
(Continued)

Cash Payments Journal

PAGE

DATE	CHQ. NO.	PAYEE	ACCOUNT DEBITED	POST REF.	DEBITS		CREDITS	
					OTHER ACCOUNTS	ACCOUNTS PAYABLE	INVENTORY	CASH

NAME
SECTION
DATE

P7-6A

Requirements 1 & 4

General Ledger

Account:					Account No.
Date	Item	Jrnl. Ref.	Debit	Credit	Balance

Account:					Account No.
Date	Item	Jrnl. Ref.	Debit	Credit	Balance

Account:					Account No.
Date	Item	Jrnl. Ref.	Debit	Credit	Balance

Account:					Account No.
Date	Item	Jrnl. Ref.	Debit	Credit	Balance

NAME
SECTION
DATE

P7-6A
(Continued)

Requirements 1 & 4 (Continued)

Account:					Account No.
Date	Item	Jrnl. Ref.	Debit	Credit	Balance

Account:					Account No.
Date	Item	Jrnl. Ref.	Debit	Credit	Balance

Account:					Account No.
Date	Item	Jrnl. Ref.	Debit	Credit	Balance

Account:					Account No.
Date	Item	Jrnl. Ref.	Debit	Credit	Balance

NAME
SECTION
DATE

Requirements 1 & 4

P7-6A

(Continued)

Account:						Account No.
Date		Item	Jrnl. Ref.	Debit	Credit	Balance

Account:						Account No.
Date		Item	Jrnl. Ref.	Debit	Credit	Balance

Account:						Account No.
Date		Item	Jrnl. Ref.	Debit	Credit	Balance

Account:						Account No.
Date		Item	Jrnl. Ref.	Debit	Credit	Balance

Account:						Account No.
Date		Item	Jrnl. Ref.	Debit	Credit	Balance

NAME
SECTION
DATE

P7-6A
(Continued)

Requirements 1 & 4

Account:						Account No.
Date		Item	Jrnl. Ref.	Debit	Credit	Balance

Requirements 2 & 4

Accounts Receivable Subsidiary Ledger

Account:						Account No.
Date		Item	Jrnl. Ref.	Debit	Credit	Balance

Account:						Account No.
Date		Item	Jrnl. Ref.	Debit	Credit	Balance

Account:						Account No.
Date		Item	Jrnl. Ref.	Debit	Credit	Balance

NAME
SECTION
DATE

P7-6A
(Continued)

Requirements 2 & 4

Accounts Payable Subsidiary Ledger

Account:					Account No.
Date	Item	Jrnl. Ref.	Debit	Credit	Balance

Account:					Account No.
Date	Item	Jrnl. Ref.	Debit	Credit	Balance

Account:					Account No.
Date	Item	Jrnl. Ref.	Debit	Credit	Balance

NAME
SECTION
DATE

P7-6A
(Continued)

Requirements 3 & 5

Sales Journal

Page

Date		Invoice No.	Account Debited	Post. Ref.	Accounts Receivable Dr. Sales Revenue Cr.	Cost of Goods Sold Dr. Inventory Cr.

Requirement 6

NAME
SECTION
DATE

Requirements 3 – 5

P7-6A
(Continued)

Cash Receipts Journal

PAGE

DATE	DEBITS		CREDITS					COST OF GOODS SOLD Dr. INVENTORY Cr.
					OTHER ACCOUNTS			
	CASH	SALES DISCOUNTS	ACCOUNTS RECEIVABLE	SALES REVENUE	ACCOUNT TITLE	POST REF.	AMOUNT	

NAME
SECTION
DATE

Requirements 3 – 5

P7-6A
(Continued)

Purchases Journal

PAGE

				CREDITS	DEBITS				
							OTHER ACCOUNTS		
DATE	ACCOUNT CREDITED	TERMS	POST REF.	ACCOUNTS PAYABLE	INVENTORY	SUPPLIES	ACCOUNT TITLE	POST. REF.	AMOUNT

NAME
SECTION
DATE

Requirements 3 – 5

P7-6A
(Continued)

Cash Payments Journal

PAGE

DATE	CHQ. NO.	PAYEE	ACCOUNT DEBITED	POST REF.	DEBITS: OTHER ACCOUNTS	DEBITS: ACCOUNTS PAYABLE	CREDITS: INVENTORY	CREDITS: CASH

NAME
SECTION
DATE

Requirements 3 – 5

P7-6A
(Continued

General Journal

DATE	ACCOUNT TITLES AND EXPLANATION	POST REF.	DEBIT	CREDIT

NAME
SECTION
DATE

P7-1B

Requirements 1 & 2

Row Number	Column A	Column B
5	Revenues:	
6	Service revenue ⟶	
7	Rent revenue ⟶	
8		____________
9	Total revenue ⟶	
10		____________
11	Expenses:	
12	Salary expense ⟶	
13	Supplies expense ⟶	
14	Rent expense ⟶	
15	Amortization expense ⟶	
16		____________
17	Total expenses ⟶	
18		____________
19	Net income ⟶	
20		============

NAME
SECTION
DATE

Requirement 3

P7-1B
(Continued)

NAME
SECTION
DATE

Requirements 1 – 3

P7-2B

Sales Journal					
Date	Invoice No.	Account Debited	Post. Ref.	Accounts Receivable Dr. Sales Revenue Cr.	Cost of Goods Sold Dr. Inventory Cr.

NAME
SECTION
DATE

P7-2B
(Continued)

Requirements 1 – 3 (Continued)

Cash Receipts Journal

PAGE

	Debits		Credits					
					Other Accounts			
DATE	CASH	SALES DISCOUNTS	ACCOUNTS RECEIVABLE	SALES REVENUE	ACCOUNT TITLE	POST REF.	AMOUNT	COST OF GOODS SOLD Dr. INVENTORY Cr.

NAME
SECTION
DATE

Requirements 1 – 3 (Continued)

P7-2B
(Continued)

General Journal

DATE		ACCOUNT TITLES AND EXPLANATION	POST REF.	DEBIT	CREDIT

NAME
SECTION
DATE

P7-3B

Requirement 1

Requirement 2

NAME
SECTION
DATE

Requirement 3

P7-3B
(Continued)

Cash Receipts Journal

PAGE

DATE	DEBITS		CREDITS					
					OTHER ACCOUNTS			
	CASH	SALES DISCOUNTS	ACCOUNTS RECEIVABLE	SALES REVENUE	ACCOUNT TITLE	POST REF.	AMOUNT	COST OF GOODS SOLD Dr. INVENTORY Cr.

NAME
SECTION
DATE

P7-4B

Requirements 1 – 3

Purchases Journal

PAGE

DATE	ACCOUNT CREDITED	TERMS	POST REF.	CREDITS	DEBITS				
							OTHER ACCOUNTS		
				ACCOUNTS PAYABLE	INVENTORY	SUPPLIES	ACCOUNT TITLE	POST. REF.	AMOUNT

NAME
SECTION
DATE

Requirements 1 – 3 (Continued)

P7-4B
(Continued)

Cash Payments Journal

PAGE

DATE	CHQ. NO.	PAYEE	ACCOUNT DEBITED	POST REF.	DEBITS		CREDITS	
					OTHER ACCOUNTS	ACCOUNTS PAYABLE	INVENTORY	CASH

NAME
SECTION
DATE

Requirements 1 – 3 (Continued)

P7-4B
(Continued)

General Journal

DATE		ACCOUNT TITLES AND EXPLANATION	POST REF.	DEBIT	CREDIT

NAME
SECTION
DATE

P7-5B

Requirement 1

April 1

April 3

April 6

April 7

April 9

April 11

April 13

April 14

April 15

April 16

April 17

April 22

April 24

April 25

April 26

April 28

April 30

NAME
SECTION
DATE

P7-5B
(Continued)

Requirements 2 & 3

Cash Payments Journal

PAGE

DATE	CHQ. NO.	PAYEE	ACCOUNT DEBITED	POST REF.	DEBITS		CREDITS	
					OTHER ACCOUNTS	ACCOUNTS PAYABLE	INVENTORY	CASH

NAME
SECTION
DATE

P7-6B

Requirements 1 & 4

Account: Account No.

Date		Item	Jrnl. Ref.	Debit	Credit	Balance

Account: Account No.

Date		Item	Jrnl. Ref.	Debit	Credit	Balance

Account: Account No.

Date		Item	Jrnl. Ref.	Debit	Credit	Balance

Account: Account No.

Date		Item	Jrnl. Ref.	Debit	Credit	Balance

NAME
SECTION
DATE

P7-7B
(Continued)

Requirements 1 & 4 (Continued)

Account:					Account No.
Date	Item	Jrnl. Ref.	Debit	Credit	Balance

Account:					Account No.
Date	Item	Jrnl. Ref.	Debit	Credit	Balance

Account:					Account No.
Date	Item	Jrnl. Ref.	Debit	Credit	Balance

Account:					Account No.
Date	Item	Jrnl. Ref.	Debit	Credit	Balance

NAME
SECTION
DATE

Requirements 1 & 4 (Continued)

P7-6B
(Continued)

Account:						Account No.
Date		Item	Jrnl. Ref.	Debit	Credit	Balance

Account:						Account No.
Date		Item	Jrnl. Ref.	Debit	Credit	Balance

Account:						Account No.
Date		Item	Jrnl. Ref.	Debit	Credit	Balance

Account:						Account No.
Date		Item	Jrnl. Ref.	Debit	Credit	Balance

Account:						Account No.
Date		Item	Jrnl. Ref.	Debit	Credit	Balance

NAME
SECTION
DATE

P7-6B
(Continued)

Requirements 1 & 4

Account:					Account No.
Date	Item	Jrnl. Ref.	Debit	Credit	Balance

Requirements 2 & 4

Accounts Receivable Subsidiary Ledger

Account:					Account No.
Date	Item	Jrnl. Ref.	Debit	Credit	Balance

Account:					Account No.
Date	Item	Jrnl. Ref.	Debit	Credit	Balance

Account:					Account No.
Date	Item	Jrnl. Ref.	Debit	Credit	Balance

NAME
SECTION
DATE

Requirements 2 & 4

P7-6B
(Continued)

Accounts Payable Subsidiary Ledger

Account:					Account No.
Date	Item	Jrnl. Ref.	Debit	Credit	Balance

Account:					Account No.
Date	Item	Jrnl. Ref.	Debit	Credit	Balance

Account:					Account No.
Date	Item	Jrnl. Ref.	Debit	Credit	Balance

NAME
SECTION
DATE

P7-6B
(Continued)

Requirements 3 & 5

Sales Journal

Page

Date		Invoice No.	Account Debited	Post. Ref.	Accounts Receivable Dr. Sales Revenue Cr.	Cost of Goods Sold Dr. Inventory Cr.

Requirement 6

NAME
SECTION
DATE

Requirements 3 – 5

P7-6B
(Continued)

Cash Receipts Journal

PAGE

DATE	DEBITS		CREDITS					
					OTHER ACCOUNTS			
	CASH	SALES DISCOUNTS	ACCOUNTS RECEIVABLE	SALES REVENUE	ACCOUNT TITLE	POST REF.	AMOUNT	COST OF GOODS SOLD Dr. INVENTORY Cr.

NAME
SECTION
DATE

Requirements 3 – 5

P7-6B
(Continued)

Purchases Journal

PAGE

DATE	ACCOUNT CREDITED	TERMS	POST REF.	CREDITS	DEBITS				
				ACCOUNTS PAYABLE	INVENTORY	SUPPLIES	OTHER ACCOUNTS		
							ACCOUNT TITLE	POST. REF.	AMOUNT

NAME
SECTION
DATE

Requirements 3 – 5

P7-6B
(Continued)

Cash Payments Journal

PAGE

DATE	CHQ. NO.	PAYEE	ACCOUNT DEBITED	POST REF.	DEBITS		CREDITS	
					OTHER ACCOUNTS	ACCOUNTS PAYABLE	INVENTORY	CASH

NAME
SECTION
DATE

Requirements 3 – 5

P7-6B
(Continued)

General Journal

Page

DATE		ACCOUNT TITLES AND EXPLANATION	POST REF.	DEBIT	CREDIT

NAME
SECTION
DATE

P7-1C

NAME
SECTION
DATE

P7-2C

NAME
SECTION
DATE

Decision Problem 1

Sales Journal					
Date	Invoice No.	Account Debited	Post. Ref.	Accounts Receivable Dr. Sales Revenue Cr.	Cost of Goods Sold Dr. Inventory Cr.

NAME
SECTION
DATE

Decision Problem 1
(Continued)

Cash Receipts Journal

PAGE

DATE	DEBITS		CREDITS					COST OF GOODS SOLD Dr. INVENTORY Cr.
					OTHER ACCOUNTS			
	CASH	SALES DISCOUNTS	ACCOUNTS RECEIVABLE	SALES REVENUE	ACCOUNT TITLE	POST REF.	AMOUNT	

NAME
SECTION
DATE

Decision Problem 1

(Continued)

NAME
SECTION
DATE

Decision Problem 2

NAME
SECTION
DATE

Comprehensive Problem 1 for Part 1

Requirements 1, 5

Account: Account No.

Date	Item	Jrnl. Ref.	Debit	Credit	Balance

Account: Account No.

Date	Item	Jrnl. Ref.	Debit	Credit	Balance

Account: Account No.

Date	Item	Jrnl. Ref.	Debit	Credit	Balance

Account: Account No.

Date	Item	Jrnl. Ref.	Debit	Credit	Balance

Account: Account No.

Date	Item	Jrnl. Ref.	Debit	Credit	Balance

NAME
SECTION
DATE

Comprehensive Problem 1 for Part 1

(Continued)

Requirements 1, 5 (Continued)

Account: | Account No.

Date		Item	Jrnl. Ref.	Debit	Credit	Balance

Account: | Account No.

Date		Item	Jrnl. Ref.	Debit	Credit	Balance

Account: | Account No.

Date		Item	Jrnl. Ref.	Debit	Credit	Balance

Account: | Account No.

Date		Item	Jrnl. Ref.	Debit	Credit	Balance

Account: | Account No.

Date		Item	Jrnl. Ref.	Debit	Credit	Balance

SECTION
DATE

Comprehensive Problem 1 for Part 1

Requirements 1, 5 (Continued)

(Continued)

Account:						Account No.
Date		Item	Jrnl. Ref.	Debit	Credit	Balance

Account:						Account No.
Date		Item	Jrnl. Ref.	Debit	Credit	Balance

Account:						Account No.
Date		Item	Jrnl. Ref.	Debit	Credit	Balance

Account:						Account No.
Date		Item	Jrnl. Ref.	Debit	Credit	Balance

NAME
SECTION
DATE

Comprehensive Problem 1 for Part 1

(Continued)

Requirements 1, 5 (Continued)

Account: | Account No.

Date		Item	Jrnl. Ref.	Debit	Credit	Balance

Account: | Account No.

Date		Item	Jrnl. Ref.	Debit	Credit	Balance

Account: | Account No.

Date		Item	Jrnl. Ref.	Debit	Credit	Balance

Account: | Account No.

Date		Item	Jrnl. Ref.	Debit	Credit	Balance

NAME
SECTION
DATE

Comprehensive Problem 1 for Part 1

Requirements 1, 5 (Continued)

(Continued)

Account:

Account No.

Date		Item	Jrnl. Ref.	Debit	Credit	Balance

Account:

Account No.

Date		Item	Jrnl. Ref.	Debit	Credit	Balance

Account:

Account No.

Date		Item	Jrnl. Ref.	Debit	Credit	Balance

NAME
SECTION
DATE

Comprehensive Problem 1 for Part 1

(Continued)

Requirements 1, 5 (Continued)

Account:						Account No.
Date		Item	Jrnl. Ref.	Debit	Credit	Balance

Account:						Account No.
Date		Item	Jrnl. Ref.	Debit	Credit	Balance

Requirement 2

The foldout worksheet to solve this problem can be found in the back of the book.

NAME
SECTION
DATE

Comprehensive Problem 1 for Part 1

Requirement 3

(Continued)

NAME
SECTION
DATE

Comprehensive Problem 1 for Part 1

(Continued)

Requirement 3 (Continued)

NAME
SECTION
DATE

Comprehensive Problem 1 for Part 1

Requirement 3 (Continued)

(Continued)

NAME
SECTION
DATE

Comprehensive Problem 1 for Part 1

Requirement 4

(Continued)

General Journal

DATE	ACCOUNT TITLES AND EXPLANATION	POST REF.	DEBIT	CREDIT

NAME
SECTION
DATE

Comprehensive Problem 1 for Part 1

Requirement 4 (Continued)

(Continued)

General Journal

DATE		ACCOUNT TITLES AND EXPLANATION	POST REF.	DEBIT	CREDIT

NAME
SECTION
DATE

Comprehensive Problem 1 for Part 1

(Continued)

Requirement 6

Current Ratio

Debt Ratio

Gross Margin Percentage

Inventory Turnover

NAME
SECTION
DATE

Comprehensive Problem 1 for Part 1

Requirement 6 (Continued)

(Continued)

NAME
SECTION
DATE

Comprehensive Problem 2 for Part 1

Requirements 1, 3 & 6

Account:					Account No.

Date		Item	Jrnl. Ref.	Debit	Credit	Balance

Account:					Account No.

Date		Item	Jrnl. Ref.	Debit	Credit	Balance

Account:					Account No.

Date		Item	Jrnl. Ref.	Debit	Credit	Balance

NAME
SECTION
DATE

Comprehensive Problem 2 for Part 1

Requirements 1, 3 & 6 (Continued)

(Continued)

Account: Account No.

Date		Item	Jrnl. Ref.	Debit	Credit	Balance

Account: Account No.

Date		Item	Jrnl. Ref.	Debit	Credit	Balance

Account: Account No.

Date		Item	Jrnl. Ref.	Debit	Credit	Balance

Account: Account No.

Date		Item	Jrnl. Ref.	Debit	Credit	Balance

NAME
SECTION
DATE

Comprehensive Problem 2 for Part 1

Requirements 1, 3 & 6 (Continued)

(Continued)

Account: | | | | | Account No.

Date		Item	Jrnl. Ref.	Debit	Credit	Balance

Account: | | | | | Account No.

Date		Item	Jrnl. Ref.	Debit	Credit	Balance

Account: | | | | | Account No.

Date		Item	Jrnl. Ref.	Debit	Credit	Balance

Account: | | | | | Account No.

Date		Item	Jrnl. Ref.	Debit	Credit	Balance

NAME
SECTION
DATE

Comprehensive Problem 2 for Part 1

Requirements 1, 3 & 6 (Continued)

(Continued)

Account: Account No.

Date		Item	Jrnl. Ref.	Debit	Credit	Balance

Account: Account No.

Date		Item	Jrnl. Ref.	Debit	Credit	Balance

Account: Account No.

Date		Item	Jrnl. Ref.	Debit	Credit	Balance

Account: Account No.

Date		Item	Jrnl. Ref.	Debit	Credit	Balance

NAME
SECTION
DATE

Comprehensive Problem 2 for Part 1

Requirements 1, 3, & 6 (Continued)

(Continued)

Account: | | | | | Account No.

Date		Item	Jrnl. Ref.	Debit	Credit	Balance

Account: | | | | | Account No.

Date		Item	Jrnl. Ref.	Debit	Credit	Balance

Account: | | | | | Account No.

Date		Item	Jrnl. Ref.	Debit	Credit	Balance

Account: | | | | | Account No.

Date		Item	Jrnl. Ref.	Debit	Credit	Balance

NAME
SECTION
DATE

Comprehensive Problem 2 for Part 1

Requirements 1, 3, & 6 (Continued)

(Continued)

Account: Account No.

Date		Item	Jrnl. Ref.	Debit	Credit	Balance

Account: Account No.

Date		Item	Jrnl. Ref.	Debit	Credit	Balance

Account: Account No.

Date		Item	Jrnl. Ref.	Debit	Credit	Balance

NAME
SECTION
DATE

Comprehensive Problem 2 for Part 1

Requirements 1, 3, & 6 (Continued)

(Continued)

Account:					Account No.
Date		Item	Jrnl. Ref.	Debit	Credit	Balance

Account:					Account No.
Date		Item	Jrnl. Ref.	Debit	Credit	Balance

Account:					Account No.
Date		Item	Jrnl. Ref.	Debit	Credit	Balance

Account:					Account No.
Date		Item	Jrnl. Ref.	Debit	Credit	Balance

NAME
SECTION
DATE

Comprehensive Problem 2 for Part 1

Requirements 1, 3, & 6 (Continued)

(Continued)

Account:						Account No.
Date		Item	Jrnl. Ref.	Debit	Credit	Balance

Account:						Account No.
Date		Item	Jrnl. Ref.	Debit	Credit	Balance

Account:						Account No.
Date		Item	Jrnl. Ref.	Debit	Credit	Balance

NAME
SECTION
DATE

Comprehensive Problem 2 for Part 1

Requirements 1 & 3

(Continued)

ACCOUNTS RECEIVABLE SUBSIDIARY LEDGER

Account:					Account No.
Date	Item	Jrnl. Ref.	Debit	Credit	Balance

Account:					Account No.
Date	Item	Jrnl. Ref.	Debit	Credit	Balance

Account:					Account No.
Date	Item	Jrnl. Ref.	Debit	Credit	Balance

Account:					Account No.
Date	Item	Jrnl. Ref.	Debit	Credit	Balance

NAME
SECTION
DATE

Comprehensive Problem 2 for Part 1

Requirements 1 & 3 (Continued)

(Continued)

ACCOUNTS PAYABLE SUBSIDIARY LEDGER

Account:					Account No.
Date	Item	Jrnl. Ref.	Debit	Credit	Balance

Account:					Account No.
Date	Item	Jrnl. Ref.	Debit	Credit	Balance

Account:					Account No.
Date	Item	Jrnl. Ref.	Debit	Credit	Balance

Account:					Account No.
Date	Item	Jrnl. Ref.	Debit	Credit	Balance

NAME
SECTION
DATE

Comprehensive Problem 2 for Part 1

Requirements 2 & 3

(Continued)

(Alternate working papers for special journals can be found after General Journal pages.)

General Journal

P. 9

DATE	ACCOUNT TITLES AND EXPLANATION	POST REF.	DEBIT	CREDIT

NAME
SECTION
DATE

Comprehensive Problem 2 for Part 1

Requirements 2 & 3 (Continued)

(Continued)

General Journal

P. 9

DATE		ACCOUNT TITLES AND EXPLANATION	POST REF.	DEBIT	CREDIT

NAME
SECTION
DATE

Comprehensive Problem 2 for Part 1

Requirements 2 & 3 (Continued)

(Continued)

General Journal

P. 9

DATE		ACCOUNT TITLES AND EXPLANATION	POST REF.	DEBIT	CREDIT

NAME
SECTION
DATE

Comprehensive Problem 2 for Part 1

Requirements 2 & 3 (Continued)

(Continued)

General Journal

P. 9

DATE		ACCOUNT TITLES AND EXPLANATION	POST REF.	DEBIT	CREDIT

NAME
SECTION
DATE

Comprehensive Problem 2 for Part 1

Requirement 2 (Continued)

(Continued)

(Alternate Working Papers)

Sales Journal					P. 4
Date	Invoice No.	Account Debited	Post. Ref.	Accounts Receivable Dr. Sales Revenue Cr.	Cost of Goods Sold Dr. Inventory Cr.

NAME
SECTION
DATE

Comprehensive Problem 2 for Part 1

Requirements 2 & 3 (Continued)

(Continued)

(Alternate Working Papers)

Cash Receipts Journal

	DEBITS		CREDITS					PAGE 11
					OTHER ACCOUNTS			
DATE	CASH	SALES DISCOUNTS	ACCOUNTS RECEIVABLE	SALES REVENUE	ACCOUNT TITLE	POST REF.	AMOUNT	COST OF GOODS SOLD Dr. INVENTORY Cr.

NAME
SECTION
DATE

Comprehensive Problem 2 for Part 1

Requirements 2 & 3 (Continued)

(Continued)

(Alternate Working Papers)

Purchases Journal

PAGE 8

				CREDITS	DEBITS				
							OTHER ACCOUNTS		
DATE	ACCOUNT CREDITED	TERMS	POST REF.	ACCOUNTS PAYABLE	INVENTORY	SUPPLIES	ACCOUNT TITLE	POST. REF.	AMOUNT

NAME
SECTION
DATE

Comprehensive Problem 2 for Part 1

(Continued)

Requirements 2 & 3 (Continued)

(Alternate Working Papers)

Cash Payments Journal

PAGE 5

DATE	CHQ. NO.	PAYEE	ACCOUNT DEBITED	POST REF.	DEBITS		CREDITS	
					OTHER ACCOUNTS	ACCOUNTS PAYABLE	INVENTORY	CASH

NAME
SECTION
DATE

Comprehensive Problem 2 for Part 1 *(Continued)*

Requirements 2, 3, & 7 (Continued)

General Journal

P. 9

DATE		ACCOUNT TITLES AND EXPLANATION	POST REF.	DEBIT	CREDIT

NAME
SECTION
DATE

Comprehensive Problem 2 for Part 1

Requirements 2, 3, & 7 (Continued)

(Continued)

General Journal

P. 9

DATE		ACCOUNT TITLES AND EXPLANATION	POST REF.	DEBIT	CREDIT

NAME
SECTION
DATE

Comprehensive Problem 2 for Part 1

Requirements 2, 3, & 7 (Continued)

(Continued)

General Journal

P. 9

DATE		ACCOUNT TITLES AND EXPLANATION	POST REF.	DEBIT	CREDIT

NAME
SECTION
DATE

Comprehensive Problem 2 for Part 1

Requirement 4 *(Continued)*

The foldout work sheet to solve this problem can be found in the back of the book.

Requirement 5

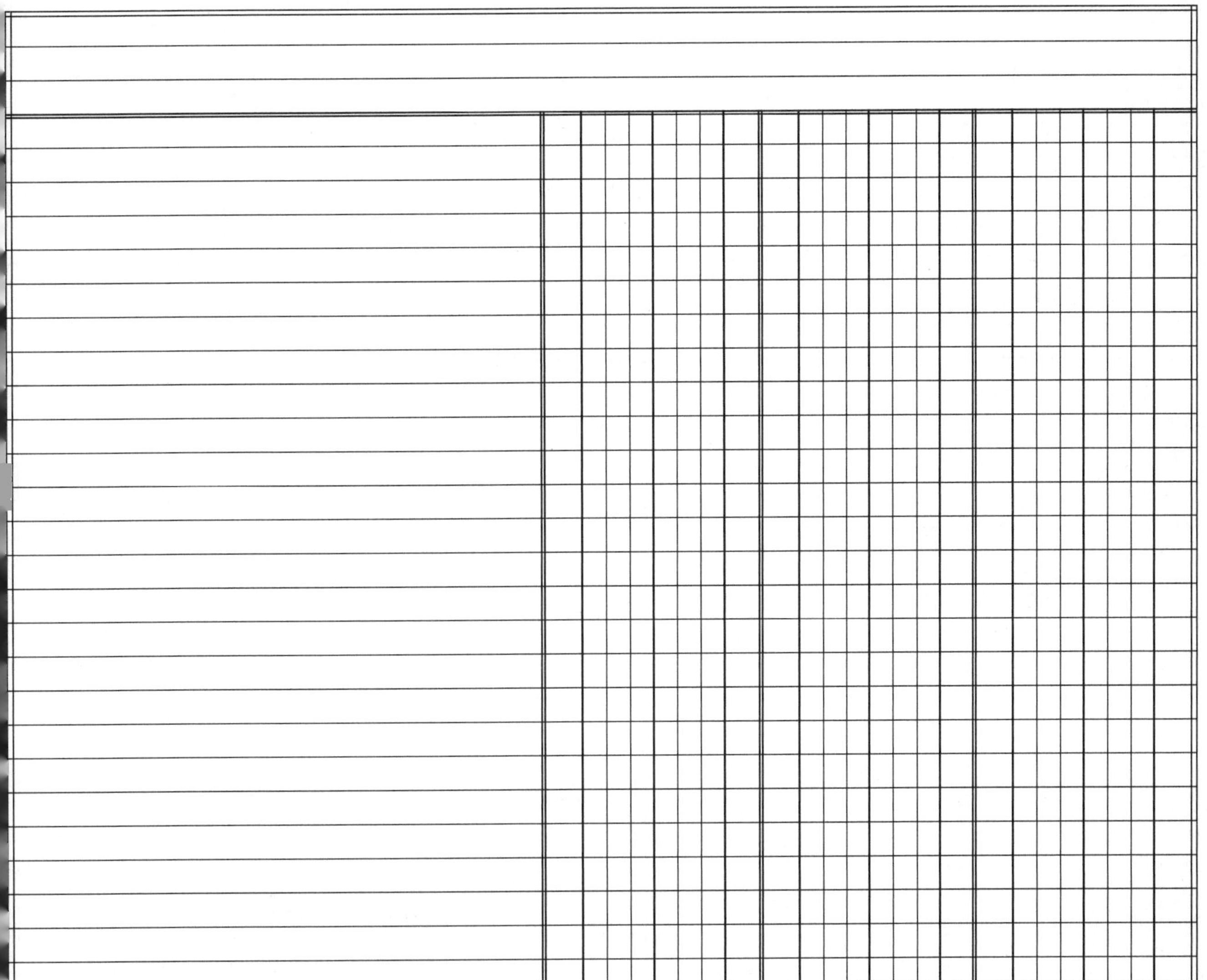

NAME
SECTION
DATE

Comprehensive Problem 2 for Part 1

Requirement 5 (Continued)

(Continued)

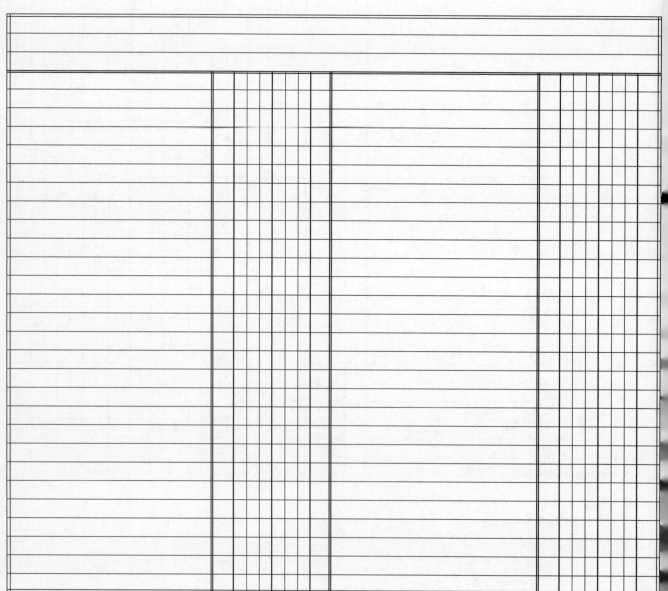

NAME
SECTION
DATE

Comprehensive Problem 2 for Part 1

Requirement 7

(Continued)

ACCOUNT	DEBIT	CREDIT

NAME
SECTION
DATE

Chapter 8

E8-1

E8-2

NAME
SECTION
DATE

E8–3

NAME
SECTION
DATE

E8–4

NAME
SECTION
DATE

E8-5

a. – f.

NAME
SECTION
DATE

E8-6

a. – e.

E8-7

Situations 1 - 4

NAME
SECTION
DATE

E8-7

Situations 1 – 4, continued

E8-8

1.

2.

3.

4.

5.

6.

7.

NAME
SECTION
DATE

E8-9

NAME
SECTION
DATE

E8-10

NAME
SECTION
DATE

E8-11

General Journal

DATE		ACCOUNT TITLES AND EXPLANATION	POST REF.	DEBIT	CREDIT

AME
ECTION
ATE

E8-12

E8-13

NAME
SECTION
DATE

E8-14

General Journal

DATE		ACCOUNT TITLES AND EXPLANATION	POST REF.	DEBIT	CREDIT

NAME
SECTION
DATE

E8-15

Requirement 1

General Journal

DATE	ACCOUNT TITLES AND EXPLANATION	POST REF.	DEBIT	CREDIT

Requirements 2 & 3

NAME
SECTION
DATE

E8-16

NAME
SECTION
DATE

Beyond the Numbers 8-1

NAME
SECTION
DATE

Beyond the Numbers 8-1

(Continued)

NAME
SECTION
DATE

Ethical Issue

Requirements 1 & 2

NAME
SECTION
DATE

P8-1A

NAME
SECTION
DATE

P8-2A

a. – e.

Requirement 1 **MISSING INTERNAL CONTROL CHARACTERISTIC**	Requirement 2 **POSSIBLE PROBLEM**	Requirement 3 **SOLUTION**

NAME
SECTION
DATE

P8-3A

Requirement 1

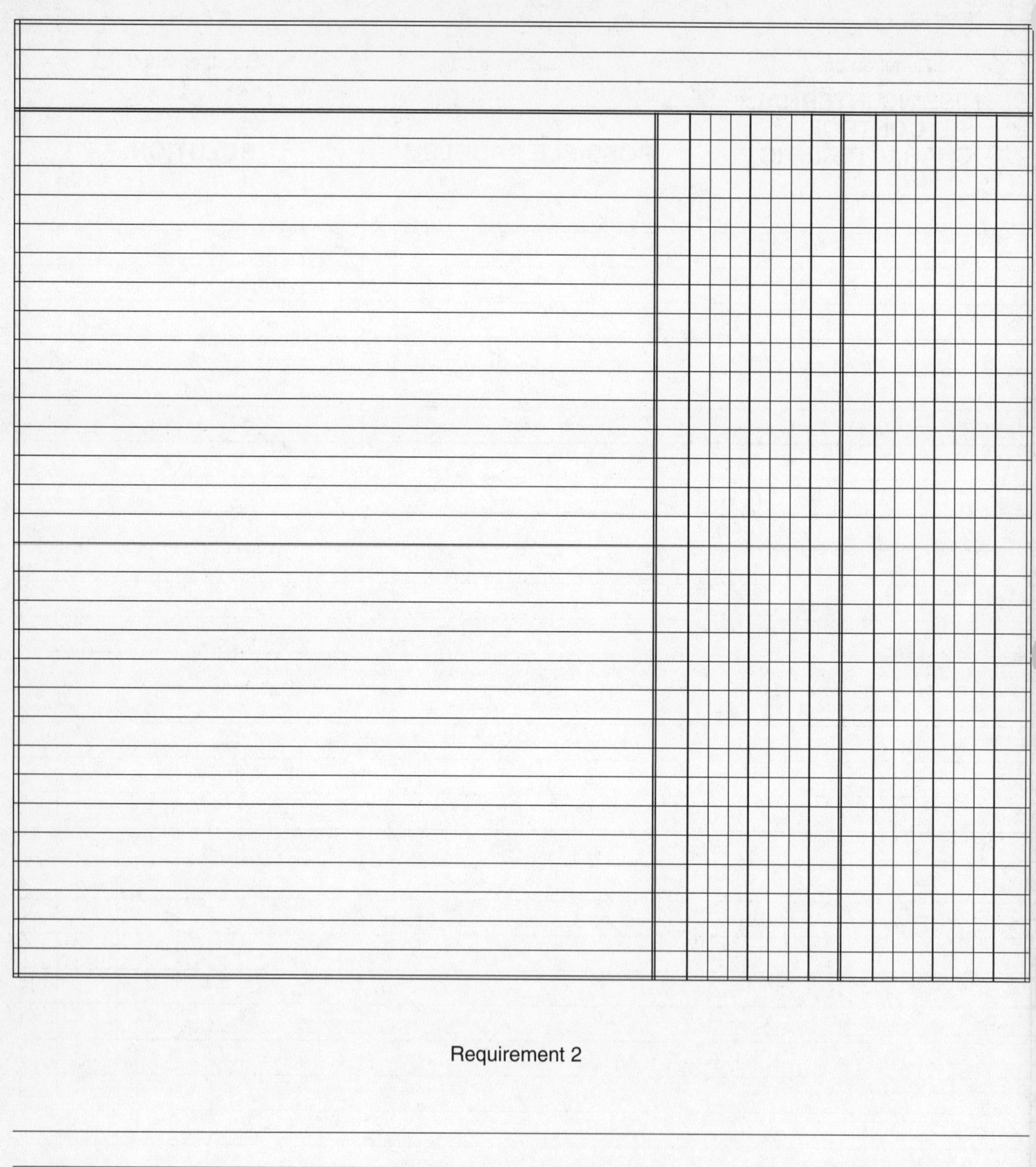

Requirement 2

NAME
SECTION
DATE

P8-4A

Requirement 1

NAME
SECTION
DATE

Requirement 2

P8-4A
(Continued)

General Journal

DATE	ACCOUNT TITLES AND EXPLANATION	POST REF.	DEBIT	CREDIT

NAME
SECTION
DATE

P8-5A

NAME
SECTION
DATE

P8-6A

NAME
SECTION
DATE

P8-7A

Requirement 1

Requirement 2

General Journal					
DATE		ACCOUNT TITLES AND EXPLANATION	POST REF.	DEBIT	CREDIT

NAME
SECTION
DATE

P8-7A
(Continued)

Requirement 2, continued

General Journal

DATE		DESCRIPTION	POST REF.	DEBIT	CREDIT

Requirement 3

General Journal

DATE		DESCRIPTION	POST REF.	DEBIT	CREDIT

NAME
SECTION
DATE

P8-8A

Requirement 1

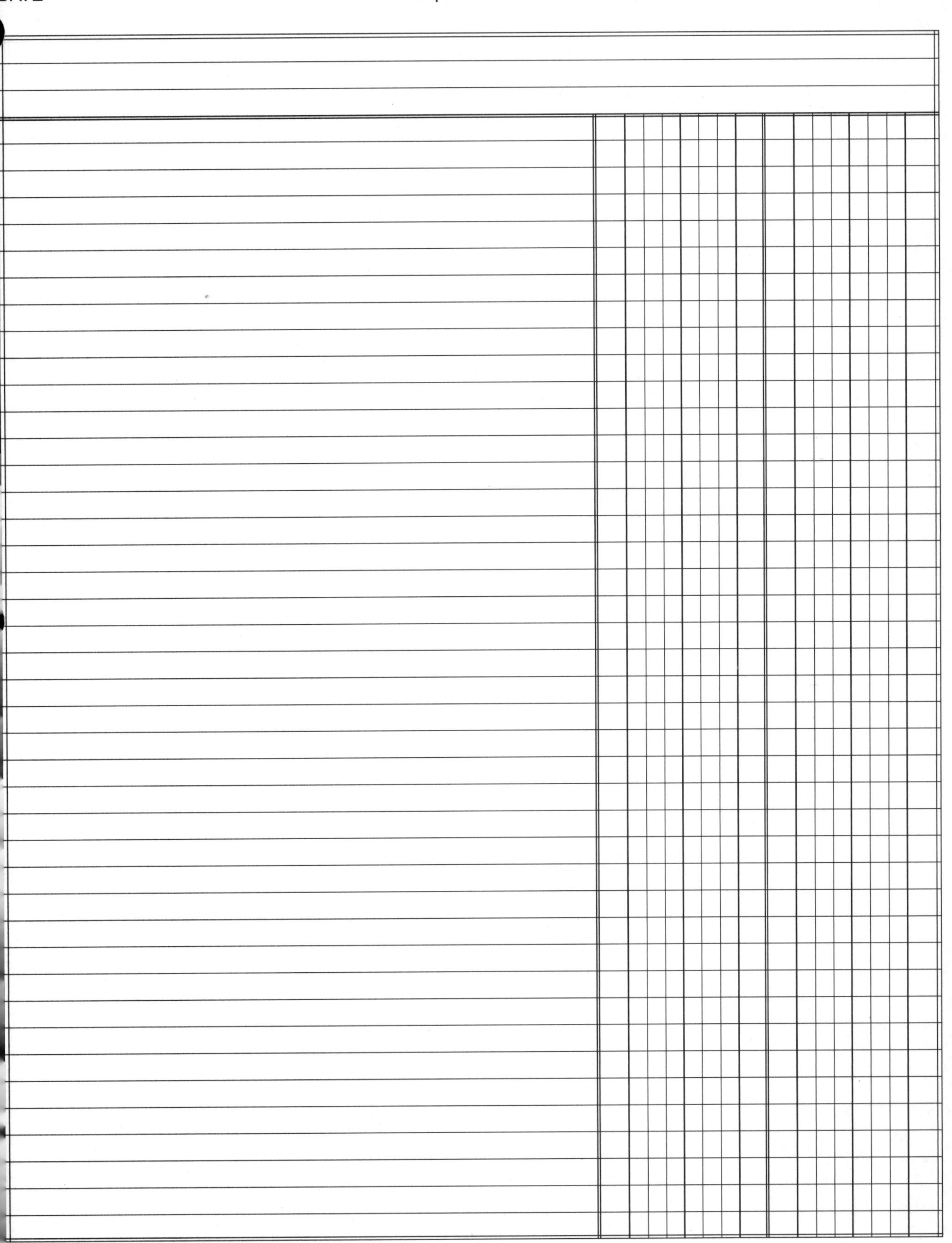

NAME
SECTION
DATE

Requirement 2

P8-8A
(Continued)

General Journal

DATE		ACCOUNT TITLES AND EXPLANATION	POST REF.	DEBIT	CREDIT

NAME
SECTION
DATE

P8-9A

NAME
SECTION
DATE

P8-1E

NAME
SECTION
DATE

P8-2B

Requirement 1 **MISSING INTERNAL CONTROL CHARACTERISTIC**	Requirement 2 **POSSIBLE PROBLEM**	Requirement 3 **SOLUTION**

NAME
SECTION
DATE

P8-3B

Requirement 1

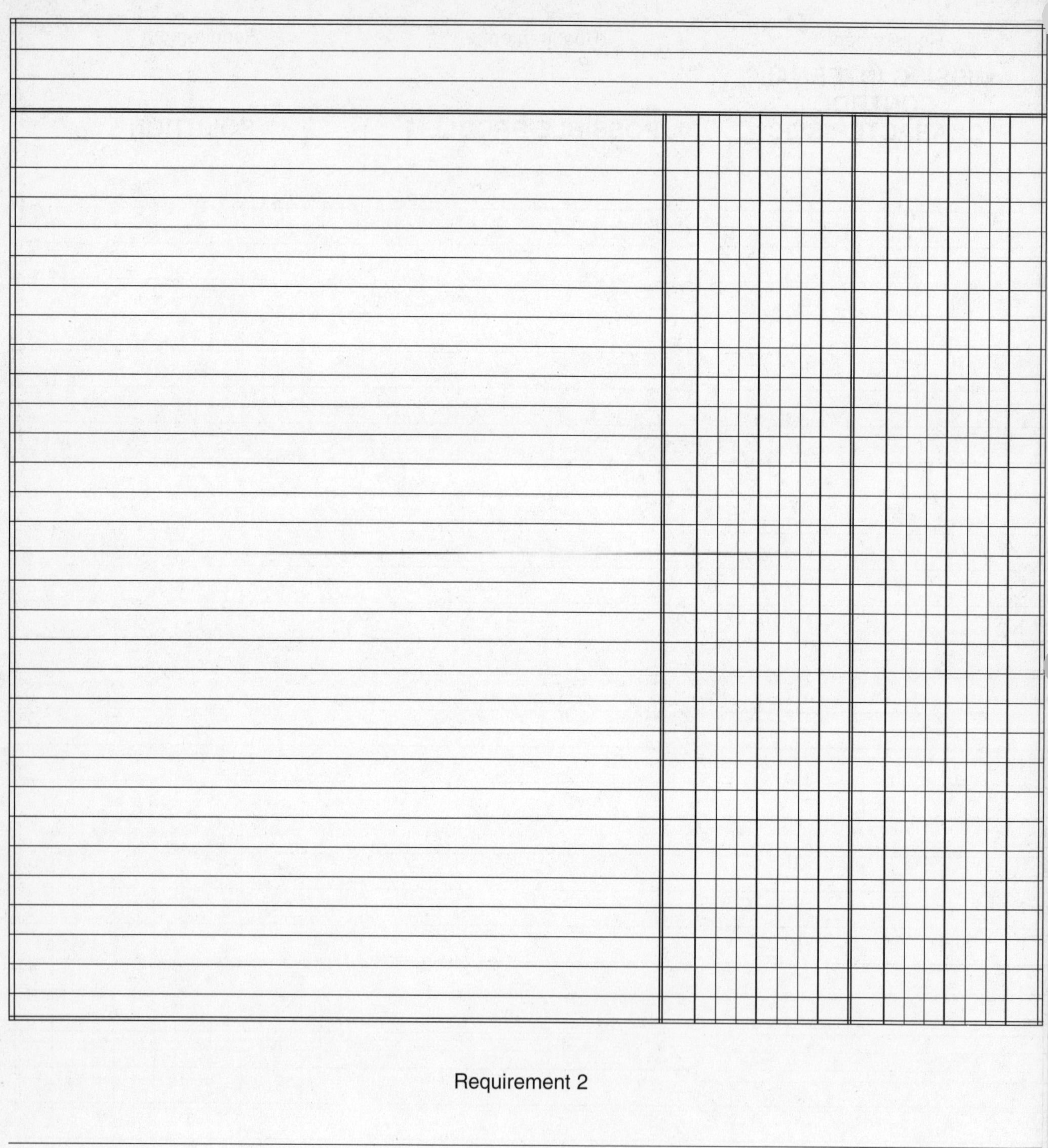

Requirement 2

NAME
SECTION
DATE

P8-4B

Requirement 1

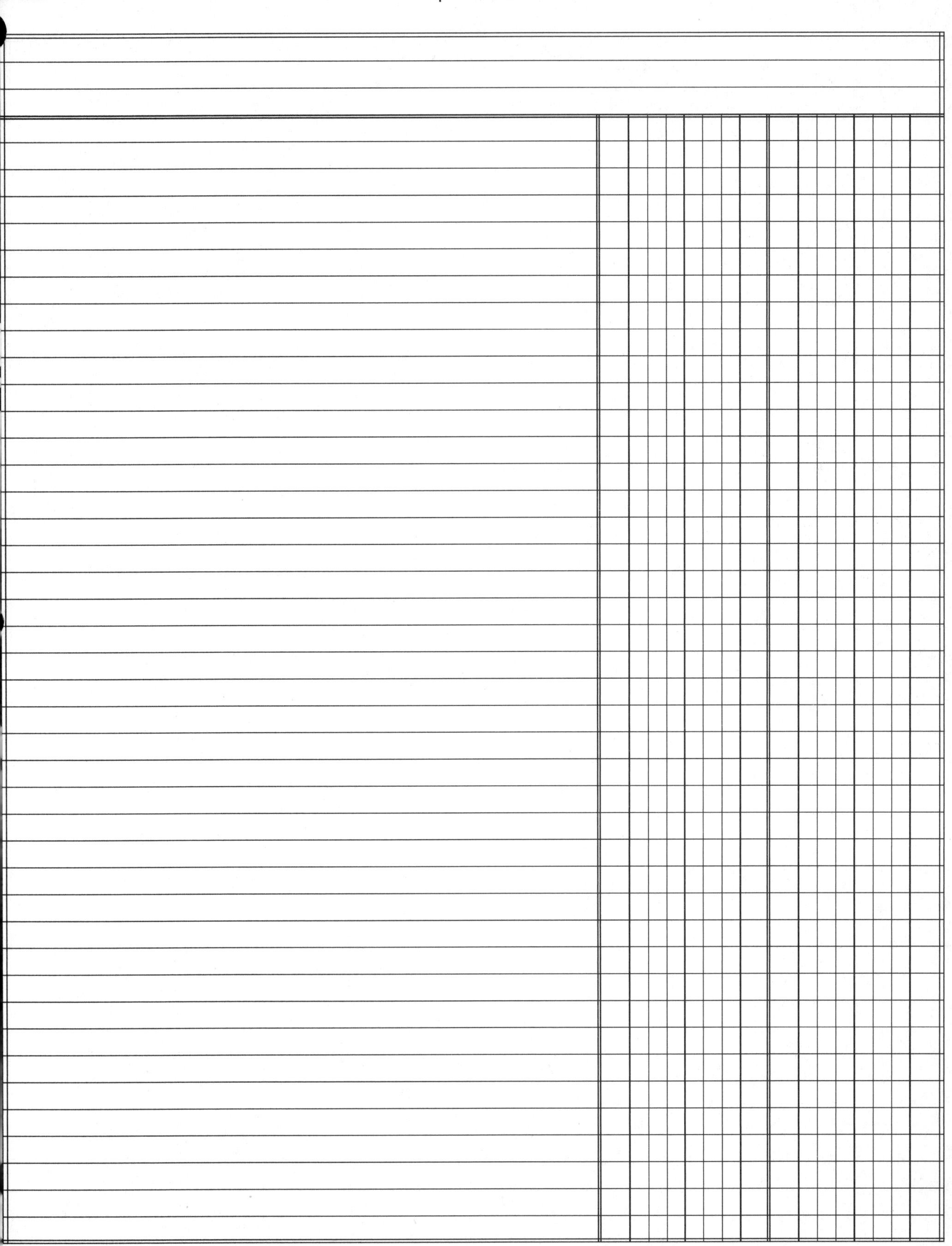

NAME
SECTION
DATE

P8-4B
(Continued)

Requirement 2

General Journal				
DATE	ACCOUNT TITLES AND EXPLANATION	POST REF.	DEBIT	CREDIT

AME
ECTION
ATE

P8-5B

NAME
SECTION
DATE

P8-6B

NAME
SECTION
DATE

P8-7B

Requirement 1

Requirement 2

General Journal

DATE		ACCOUNT TITLES AND EXPLANATION	POST REF.	DEBIT	CREDIT

NAME
SECTION
DATE

P8-7B
(Continued)

Requirement 2

General Journal

DATE		ACCOUNT TITLES AND EXPLANATION	POST REF.	DEBIT	CREDIT

NAME
SECTION
DATE

P8-8B

Requirement 1

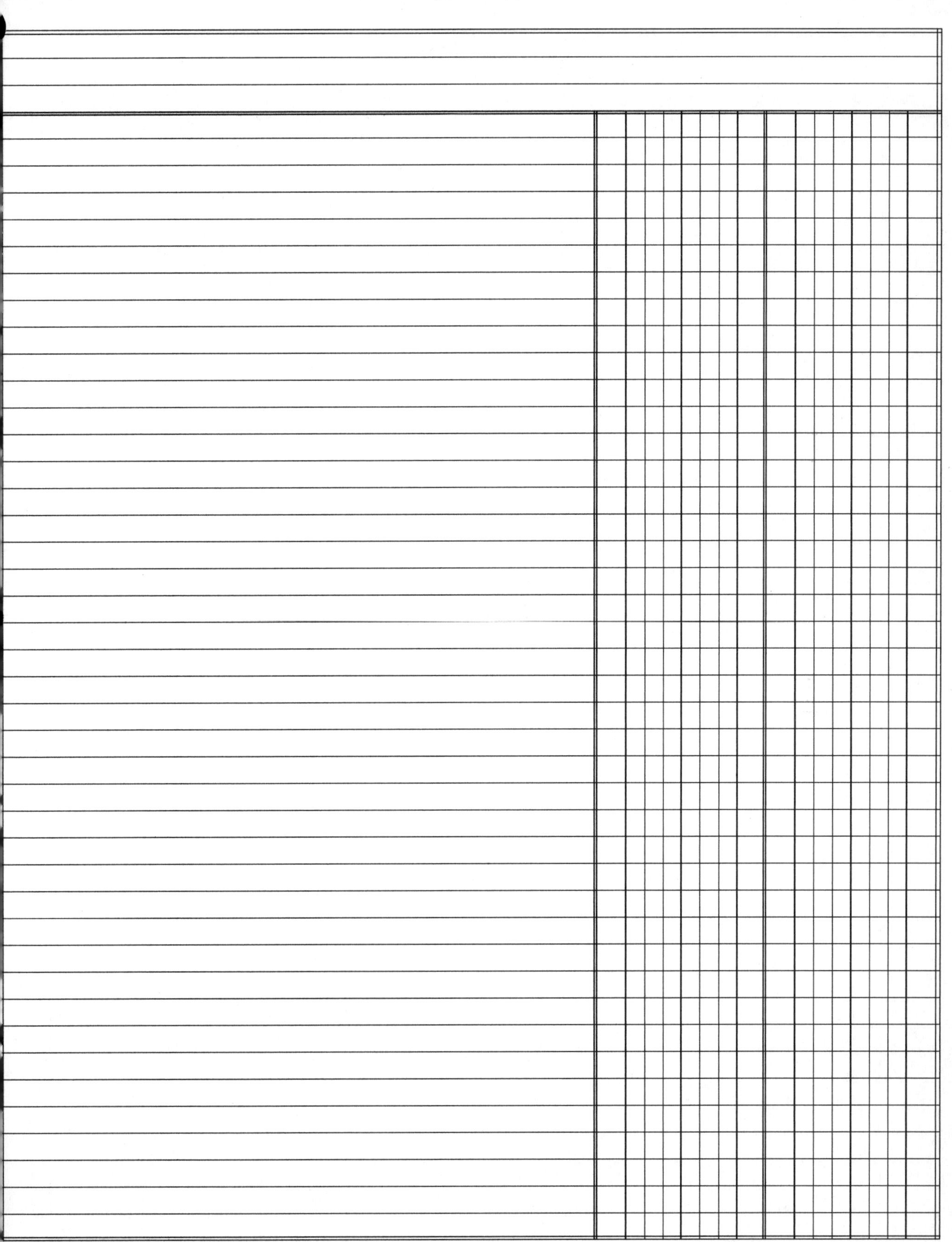

NAM
SECTION
DATE

Requirement 2

P8-8B
(Continued)

General Journal

DATE		ACCOUNT TITLES AND EXPLANATION	POST REF.	DEBIT	CREDIT

NAME
SECTION
DATE

P8-9B

NAME
SECTION
DATE

P8-1C

P8-2C

NAME
SECTION
DATE

Decision Problem

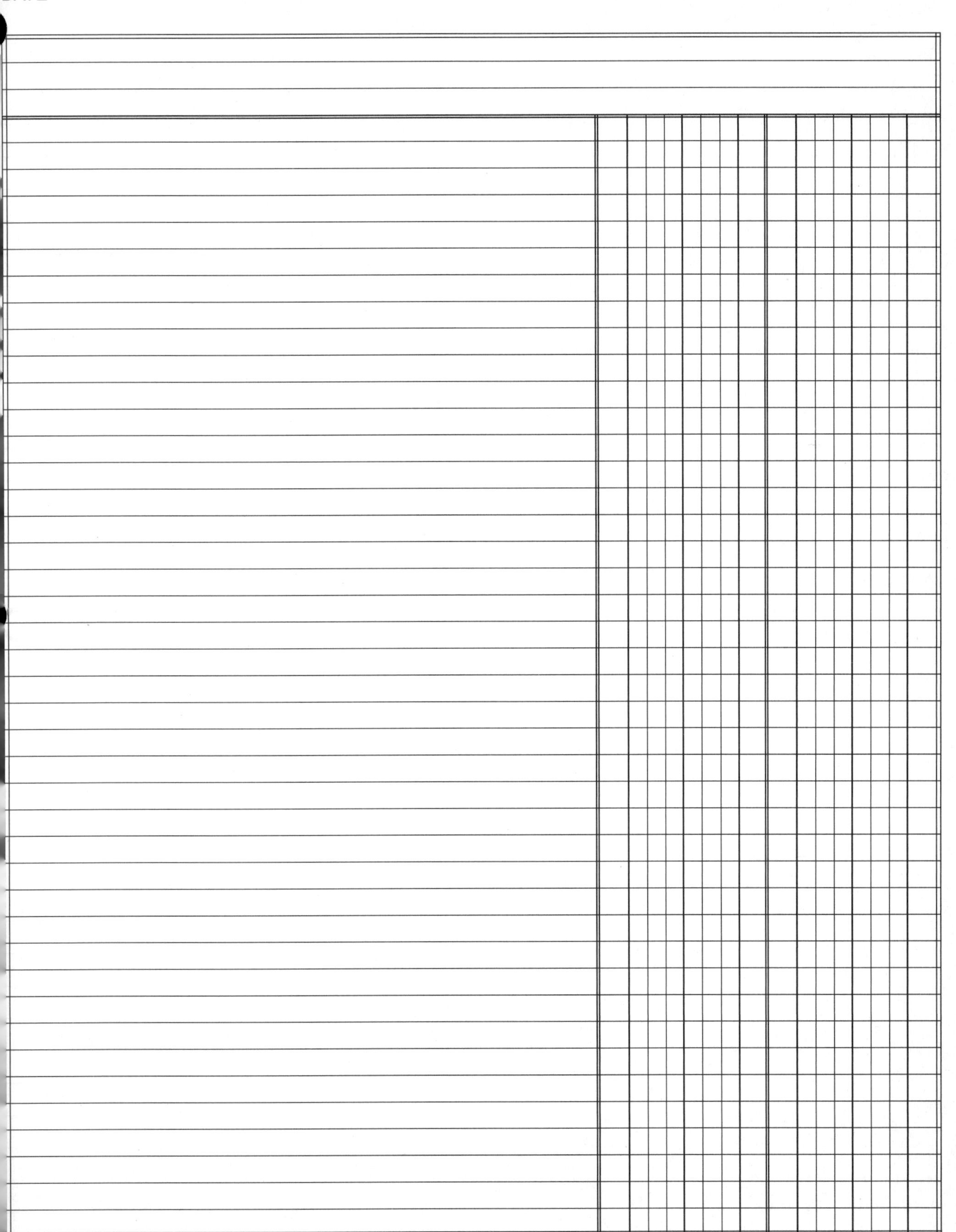

NAME
SECTION
DATE

Decision Problem

(Continued)

NAME
SECTION
DATE

Financial Statement Problem

Requirements 1 – 5

NAME
SECTION
DATE

Chapter 9

E9-1

NAME
SECTION
DATE

E9-2

Requirement 1

General Journal				
DATE	ACCOUNT TITLES AND EXPLANATION	POST REF.	DEBIT	CREDIT

Requirement 2

Requirement 3

NAME
SECTION
DATE

E9-3

Requirement 1

General Journal				
DATE	ACCOUNT TITLES AND EXPLANATION	POST REF.	DEBIT	CREDIT

Requirement 2

NAME
SECTION
DATE

E9-4

Requirement 1

General Journal				
DATE	ACCOUNT TITLES AND EXPLANATION	POST REF.	DEBIT	CREDIT

Requirements 2 & 4

NAME
SECTION
DATE

E9-4
(Continued)

Requirement 3

Aging Schedule

Requirement 4

General Journal				
DATE	ACCOUNT TITLES AND EXPLANATION	POST REF.	DEBIT	CREDIT

Requirement 5

NAME
SECTION
DATE

E9-5

Requirement 1

General Journal				
DATE	ACCOUNT TITLES AND EXPLANATION	POST REF.	DEBIT	CREDIT

Requirement 2

NAME
SECTION
DATE

E9-6

E9-7

General Journal				
DATE	ACCOUNT TITLES AND EXPLANATION	POST REF.	DEBIT	CREDIT

NAME
SECTION
DATE

E9-8

General Journal

DATE		ACCOUNT TITLES AND EXPLANATION	POST REF.	DEBIT	CREDIT

NAME
SECTION
DATE

E9-9

Requirements 1 & 2

COMPUTATIONS:

NAME
SECTION
DATE

E9-10

Requirements 1 & 2

COMPUTATIONS:

NAME
SECTION
DATE

E9-11

COMPUTATIONS:

NAME
SECTION
DATE

Beyond the Numbers 9-1

NAME
SECTION
DATE

Ethical Issue

NAME
SECTION
DATE

P9-1A

NAME
SECTION
DATE

P9-2A

Requirement 1

General Journal					
DATE		ACCOUNT TITLES AND EXPLANATION	POST REF.	DEBIT	CREDIT

Requirement 2

General Journal					
DATE		ACCOUNT TITLES AND EXPLANATION	POST REF.	DEBIT	CREDIT

NAME
SECTION
DATE

P9-2A
(Continued)

Requirement 2 (Continued)

Requirement 3

NAME
SECTION
DATE

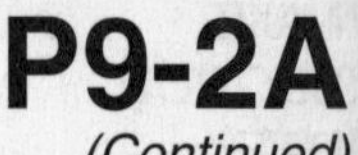

(Continued)

Requirement 4

NAME
SECTION
DATE

P9-3A

Requirement 1

General Journal

DATE		ACCOUNT TITLES AND EXPLANATION	POST REF.	DEBIT	CREDIT

NAME
SECTION
DATE

P9-3A
(Continued)

Requirement 2

Account:					Account No.
Date	Item	Jrnl. Ref.	Debit	Credit	Balance

Requirement 3

NAME
SECTION
DATE

P9-4A

Requirements 1 & 2

Account:					Account No.
Date	Item	Jrnl. Ref.	Debit	Credit	Balance

Account:					Account No.
Date	Item	Jrnl. Ref.	Debit	Credit	Balance

NAME
SECTION
DATE

Requirement 2

P9-4A
(Continued)

General Journal

DATE		ACCOUNT TITLES AND EXPLANATION	POST REF.	DEBIT	CREDIT

NAME
SECTION
DATE

P9-4A
(Continued)

Requirement 2 (Continued)

General Journal

DATE		ACCOUNT TITLES AND EXPLANATION	POST REF.	DEBIT	CREDIT

Requirement 3

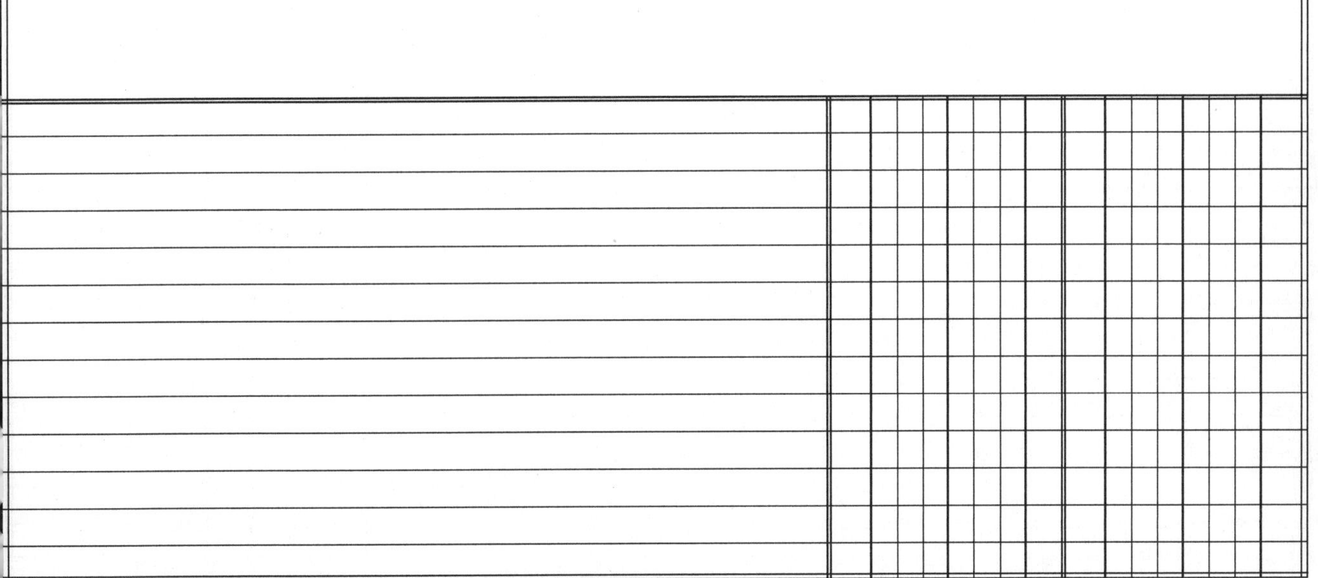

NAME
SECTION
DATE

P9-4A
(Continued)

Requirement 4a

General Journal				
DATE	ACCOUNT TITLES AND EXPLANATION	POST REF.	DEBIT	CREDIT

Requirement 4b

NAME
SECTION
DATE

P9-5A

Requirement 1

NOTE	DUE DATE	PRINCIPAL + INTEREST		MATURITY VALUE
(a)			=	
(b)			=	
(c)			=	

Requirement 2

General Journal				
DATE	ACCOUNT TITLES AND EXPLANATION	POST REF.	DEBIT	CREDIT

NAME
SECTION
DATE

P9-5A
(Continued)

Requirement 3

General Journal

DATE		ACCOUNT TITLES AND EXPLANATION	POST REF.	DEBIT	CREDIT

Requirement 4

NAME
SECTION
DATE

P9-6A

General Journal

DATE		ACCOUNT TITLES AND EXPLANATION	POST REF.	DEBIT	CREDIT

NAME
SECTION
DATE

P9-6A
(Continued)

General Journal

DATE		ACCOUNT TITLES AND EXPLANATION	POST REF.	DEBIT	CREDIT

NAME
SECTION
DATE

P9-7A

General Journal

DATE		ACCOUNT TITLES AND EXPLANATION	POST REF.	DEBIT	CREDIT

NAME
SECTION
DATE

P9-7A
(Continued)

General Journal

DATE		ACCOUNT TITLES AND EXPLANATION	POST REF.	DEBIT	CREDIT

NAME
SECTION
DATE

P9-8A

Requirement 1

	2006	2005

A. CURRENT RATIO:

B. ACID-TEST RATIO:

C. DAYS' SALES IN RECEIVABLES:

NAME
SECTION
DATE

Requirement 2

P9-8A
(Continued)

NAME
SECTION
DATE

Requirement 1

P9-9A

General Journal

DATE		ACCOUNT TITLES AND EXPLANATION	POST REF.	DEBIT	CREDIT

NAME
SECTION
DATE

P9-9A
(Continued)

Requirement 2

a)

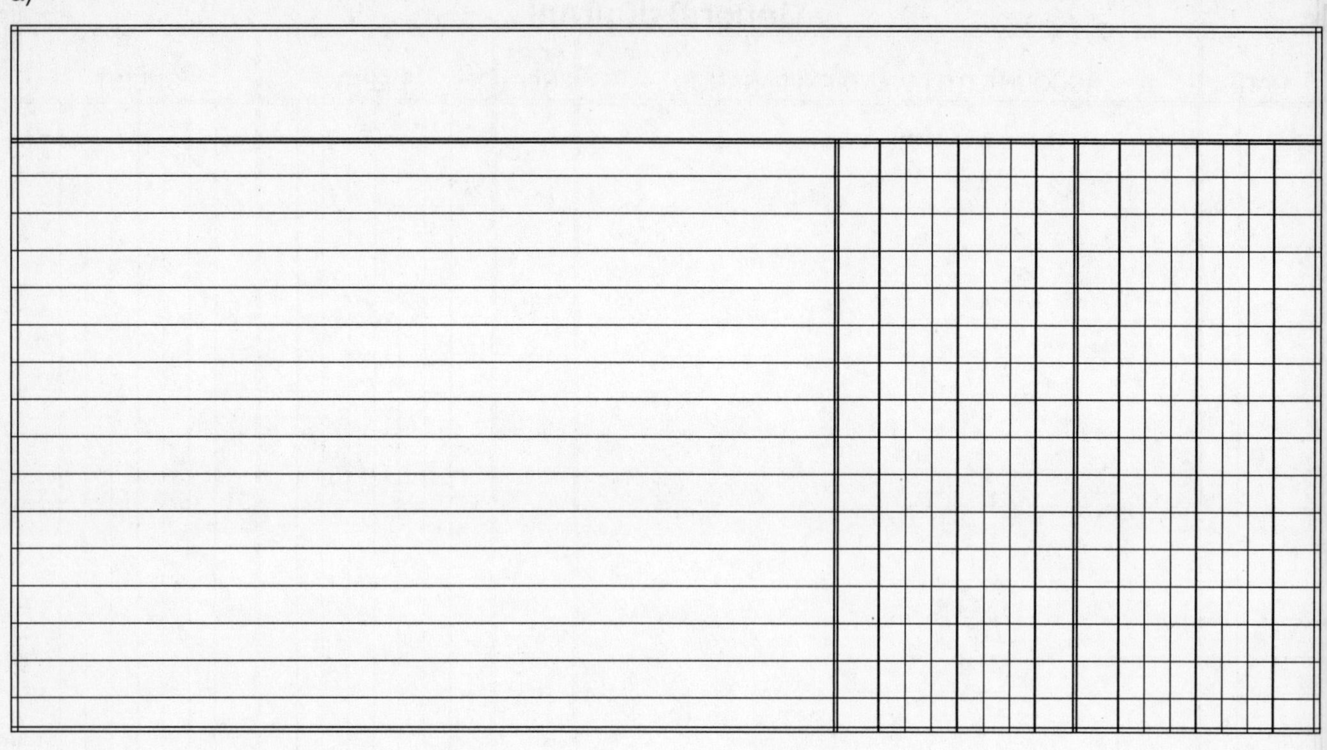

b)

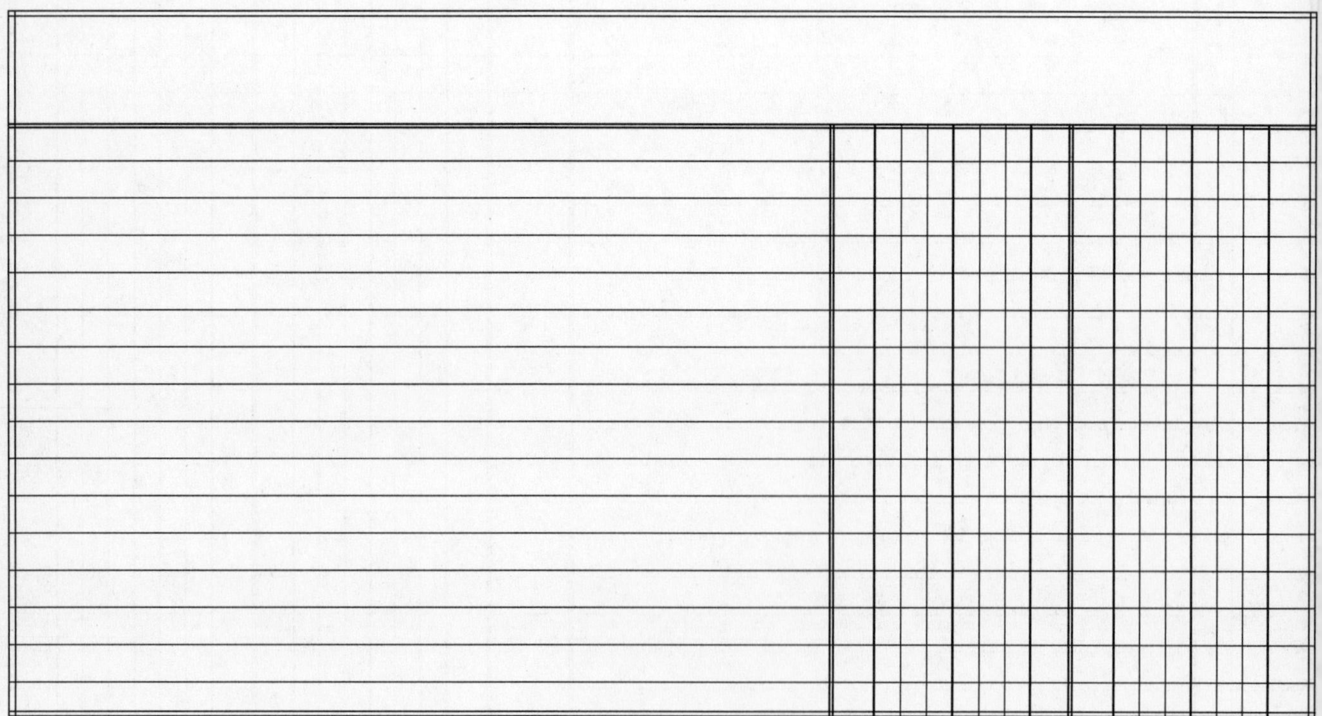

NAME
SECTION
DATE

P9-10A

Requirement 1

General Journal

DATE		ACCOUNT TITLES AND EXPLANATION	POST REF.	DEBIT	CREDIT

NAME
SECTION
DATE

P9-10A
(Continued)

Requirements 1 & 2

General Journal

DATE		ACCOUNT TITLES AND EXPLANATION	POST REF.	DEBIT	CREDIT

Requirement 3

NAME
SECTION
DATE

P9-1B

NAME
SECTION
DATE

P9-2B

Requirement 1

General Journal				
DATE	ACCOUNT TITLES AND EXPLANATION	POST REF.	DEBIT	CREDIT

NAME
SECTION
DATE

Requirement 2

P9-2B
(Continued)

General Journal

DATE		ACCOUNT TITLES AND EXPLANATION	POST REF.	DEBIT	CREDIT

NAME
SECTION
DATE

P9-2B
(Continued)

Requirement 3

Requirement 4

NAME
SECTION
DATE

P9-3B

Requirement 1

General Journal

DATE		ACCOUNT TITLES AND EXPLANATION	POST REF.	DEBIT	CREDIT

NAME
SECTION
DATE

P9-3B
(Continued)

Requirement 2

Account:					Account No.
Date	Item	Jrnl. Ref.	Debit	Credit	Balance

Requirement 3

NAME
SECTION
DATE

P9-4B

Requirements 1 & 2

Account:					Account No.
Date	Item	Jrnl. Ref.	Debit	Credit	Balance

Account:					Account No.
Date	Item	Jrnl. Ref.	Debit	Credit	Balance

NAME
SECTION
DATE

Requirement 2

P9-4B
(Continued)

General Journal

DATE		ACCOUNT TITLES AND EXPLANATION	POST REF.	DEBIT	CREDIT

Requirement 2 (Continued)

P9-4B
(Continued)

General Journal

DATE		ACCOUNT TITLES AND EXPLANATION	POST REF.	DEBIT	CREDIT

Requirement 3

NAME
SECTION
DATE

P9-4B
(Continued)

Requirement 4a

General Journal

DATE		ACCOUNT TITLES AND EXPLANATION	POST REF.	DEBIT	CREDIT

Requirement 4b

NAME
SECTION
DATE

P9-5B

Requirement 1

NOTE	DUE DATE	PRINCIPAL + INTEREST		MATURITY VALUE
(a)			=	
(b)			=	
(c)			=	
(d)			=	

Requirement 2

General Journal

DATE		ACCOUNT TITLES AND EXPLANATION	POST REF.	DEBIT	CREDIT

NAME
SECTION
DATE

Requirement 3

P9-5B
(Continued)

General Journal

DATE		ACCOUNT TITLES AND EXPLANATION	POST REF.	DEBIT	CREDIT

Requirement 4

NAME
SECTION
DATE

P9-6B

General Journal

DATE		ACCOUNT TITLES AND EXPLANATION	POST REF.	DEBIT	CREDIT

NAME
SECTION
DATE

P9-6B
(Continued)

General Journal

DATE		ACCOUNT TITLES AND EXPLANATION	POST REF.	DEBIT	CREDIT

NAME
SECTION
DATE

P9-7B

General Journal

DATE		ACCOUNT TITLES AND EXPLANATION	POST REF.	DEBIT	CREDIT

NAME
SECTION
DATE

P9-7B
(Continued)

General Journal

DATE	ACCOUNT TITLES AND EXPLANATION	POST REF.	DEBIT	CREDIT

NAME
SECTION
DATE

P9-8B

Requirement 1

	2005	2004

A. CURRENT RATIO:

B. ACID-TEST RATIO:

C. DAYS' SALES IN RECEIVABLES:

NAME
SECTION
DATE

P9-8B
(Continued

Requirement 2

NAME
SECTION
DATE

P9-9B

Requirement 1

General Journal				
DATE	ACCOUNT TITLES AND EXPLANATION	POST REF.	DEBIT	CREDIT

NAME
SECTION
DATE

P9-9B
(Continued)

Requirement 2

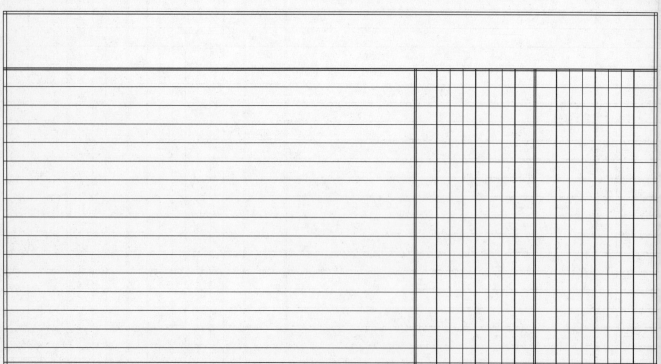

NAME
SECTION
DATE

P9-10B

Requirement 1

General Journal

DATE		ACCOUNT TITLES AND EXPLANATION	POST REF.	DEBIT	CREDIT

NAME
SECTION
DATE

P2-10B
(Continued)

Requirements 1 & 2

General Journal				
DATE	ACCOUNT TITLES AND EXPLANATION	POST REF.	DEBIT	CREDIT

Requirement 3

NAME
SECTION
DATE

P9-1C

NAME
SECTION
DATE

P9-2C

NAME
SECTION
DATE

Decision Problem 1

Requirements 1 & 2

NAME
SECTION
DATE

Decision Problem 2

Requirement 1

	2006	2005

Requirement 2

NAME
SECTION
DATE

Financial Statement Problem

Requirements 1 – 5

NAME
SECTION
DATE

Financial Statement Problem

(Continued)

Requirements 1 – 5 (Continued)

NAME
SECTION
DATE

E9-1A

E9-2A

General Journal				
DATE	ACCOUNT TITLES & EXPLANATION	POST REF.	DEBIT	CREDIT

NAME
SECTION
DATE

E9-3A

General Journal

DATE		ACCOUNT TITLES AND EXPLANATION	POST REF.	DEBIT	CREDIT

NAME
SECTION
DATE

P9-1A

Requirement 1

NOTE	DUE DATE	PRINCIPAL + INTEREST		MATURITY VALUE
(a)	______	______	=	______
(b)	______	______	=	______
(c)	______	______	=	______

Requirement 2

NOTE	MATURITY VALUE		DISCOUNT		PROCEEDS
(a)	______	–	______	=	______
(b)	______	–	______	=	______
(c)	______	–	______	=	______

Requirement 3

General Journal

DATE		ACCOUNT TITLES AND EXPLANATION	POST REF.	DEBIT	CREDIT

NAME
SECTION
DATE

P9-2A

Requirement 1

NOTE	DUE DATE	PRINCIPAL + INTEREST		MATURITY VALUE
(a)			=	
(b)			=	
(c)			=	

Requirement 2

NOTE	MATURITY VALUE		DISCOUNT		PROCEEDS
(a)		–		=	
(b)		–		=	
(c)		–		=	

Requirement 3

General Journal

DATE		ACCOUNT TITLES AND EXPLANATION	POST REF.	DEBIT	CREDIT

NAME
SECTION
DATE

Chapter 10

E10-1

NAME
SECTION
DATE

E10-2

NAME
SECTION
DATE

E10-3

General Journal

DATE		ACCOUNT TITLES AND EXPLANATION	POST REF.	DEBIT	CREDIT

COMPUTATIONS:

NAME
SECTION
DATE

E10-4

E10-5

NAME
SECTION
DATE

E10-6

Requirement 1

YEAR	STRAIGHT-LINE	UNITS-OF-PRODUCTION	DOUBLE-DECLINING BALANCE

COMPUTATIONS:

NAME
SECTION
DATE

Requirements 2 & 3

E10-6
(Continued)

E10-7

NAME
SECTION
DATE

E10-8

General Journal

DATE		ACCOUNT TITLES AND EXPLANATION	POST REF.	DEBIT	CREDIT

COMPUTATIONS:

NAME
SECTION
DATE

E10-9

General Journal

DATE		ACCOUNT TITLES AND EXPLANATION	POST REF.	DEBIT	CREDIT

COMPUTATIONS:

NAME
SECTION
DATE

E10-10

E10-11

General Journal				
DATE	ACCOUNT TITLES AND EXPLANATION	POST REF.	DEBIT	CREDIT

COMPUTATIONS:

NAME
SECTION
DATE

E10-12

Parts 1 & 2

General Journal

DATE		ACCOUNT TITLES AND EXPLANATION	POST REF.	DEBIT	CREDIT

COMPUTATIONS:

NAME
SECTION
DATE

E10-13

Requirements 1–3

NAME
SECTION
DATE

E10-14

Requirement 1

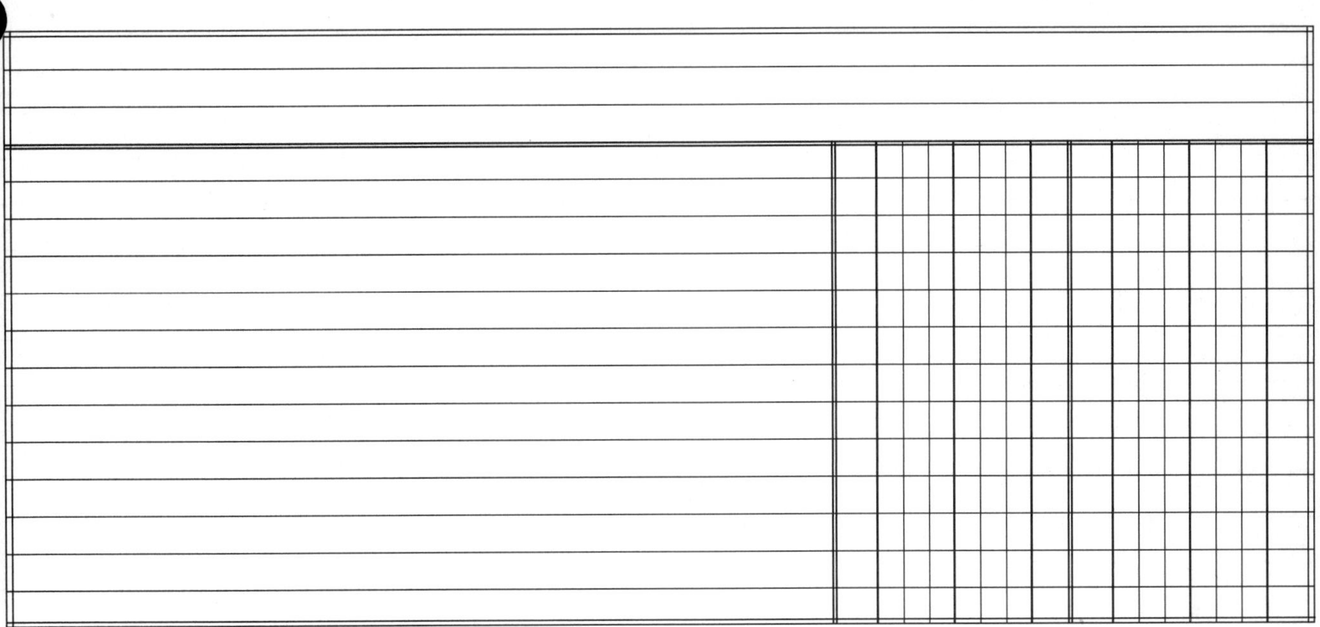

Requirement 2

General Journal				
DATE	ACCOUNT TITLES AND EXPLANATION	POST REF.	DEBIT	CREDIT

NAME
SECTION
DATE

E10-14
(Continued)

Requirement 3

Requirement 4

General Journal

DATE		DESCRIPTION	POST REF.	DEBIT	CREDIT

NAME
SECTION
DATE

E10-15

Requirement 1

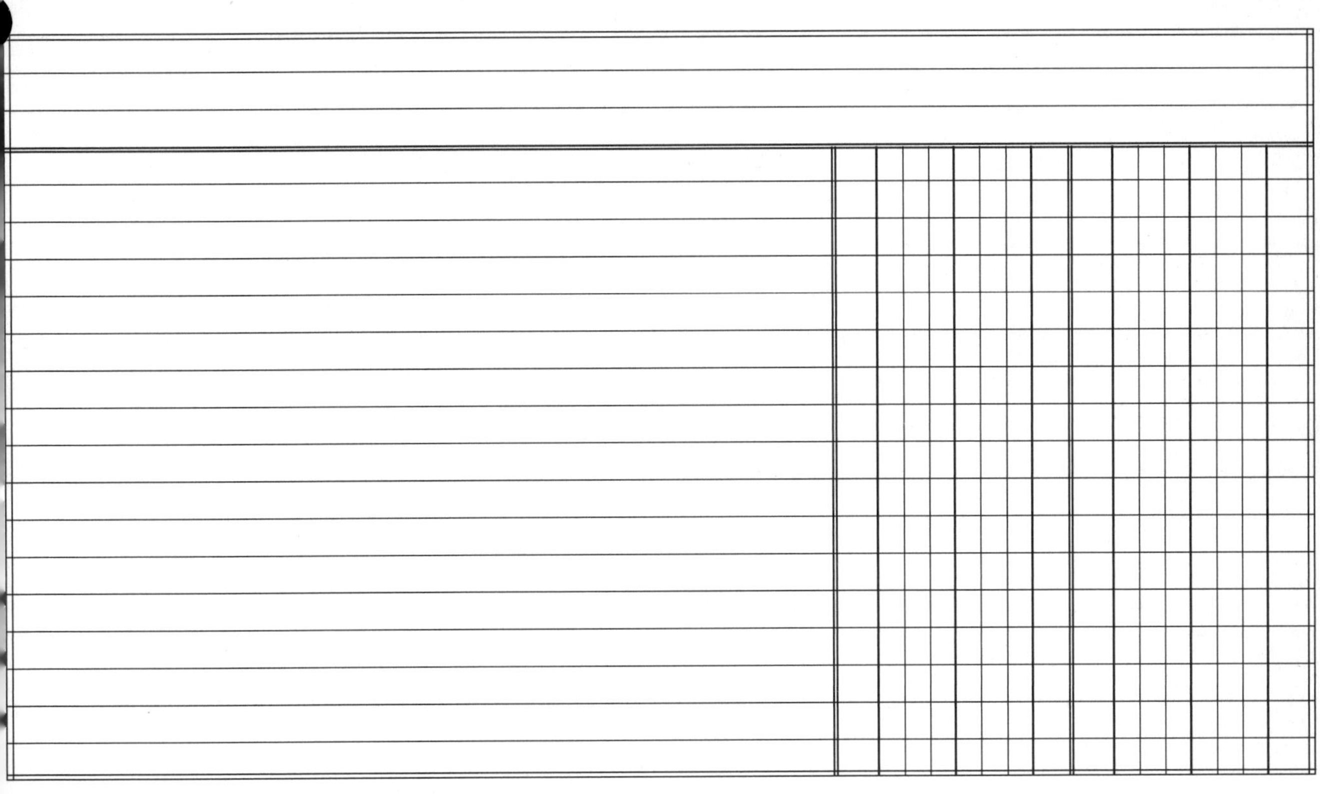

Requirement 2

General Journal

DATE		ACCOUNT TITLES AND EXPLANATION	POST REF.	DEBIT	CREDIT

NAME
SECTION
DATE

E10-15
(Continued)

Requirement 3

Requirement 4

General Journal					
DATE		DESCRIPTION	POST REF.	DEBIT	CREDIT

NAME
SECTION
DATE

E10-16

	YEAR			
	1	2	3	4

COMPUTATIONS:

NAME
SECTION
DATE

E10-17

Requirements 1 & 2

NAME
SECTION
DATE

E10-17
(Continued)

Requirement 3

General Journal				
DATE	ACCOUNT TITLES AND EXPLANATION	POST REF.	DEBIT	CREDIT

COMPUTATIONS:

NAME
SECTION
DATE

Beyond the Numbers 10-1

Situations 1 – 3

NAME
SECTION
DATE

Ethical Issue

Requirements 1 & 2

NAME
SECTION
DATE

P10-1A

Requirement 1

ITEM	LAND	LAND IMPROVEMENTS	OFFICE BUILDING	GARAGE BUILDING	FURNITURE

COMPUTATIONS:

NAME
SECTION
DATE

P10-1A
(Continued)

Requirement 2

General Journal				
DATE	ACCOUNT TITLES AND EXPLANATION	POST REF.	DEBIT	CREDIT

COMPUTATIONS:

NAME
SECTION
DATE

P10-2A

General Journal

DATE	ACCOUNT TITLES AND EXPLANATION	POST REF.	DEBIT	CREDIT

NAME
SECTION
DATE

P10-2A
(Continued)

General Journal

DATE		ACCOUNT TITLES AND EXPLANATION	POST REF.	DEBIT	CREDIT

NAME
SECTION
DATE

P10-3A

NAME
SECTION
DATE

P10-4A

Requirement 1

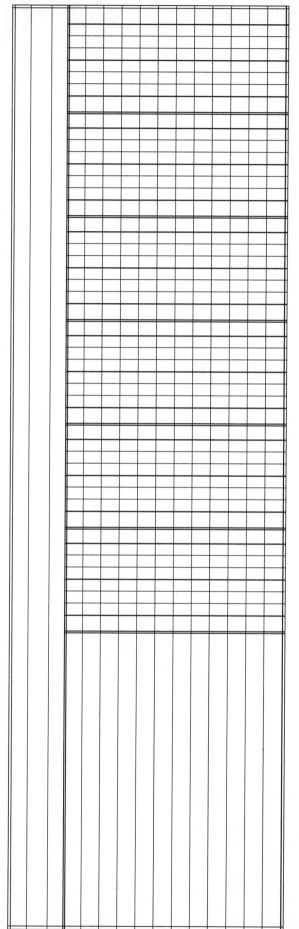

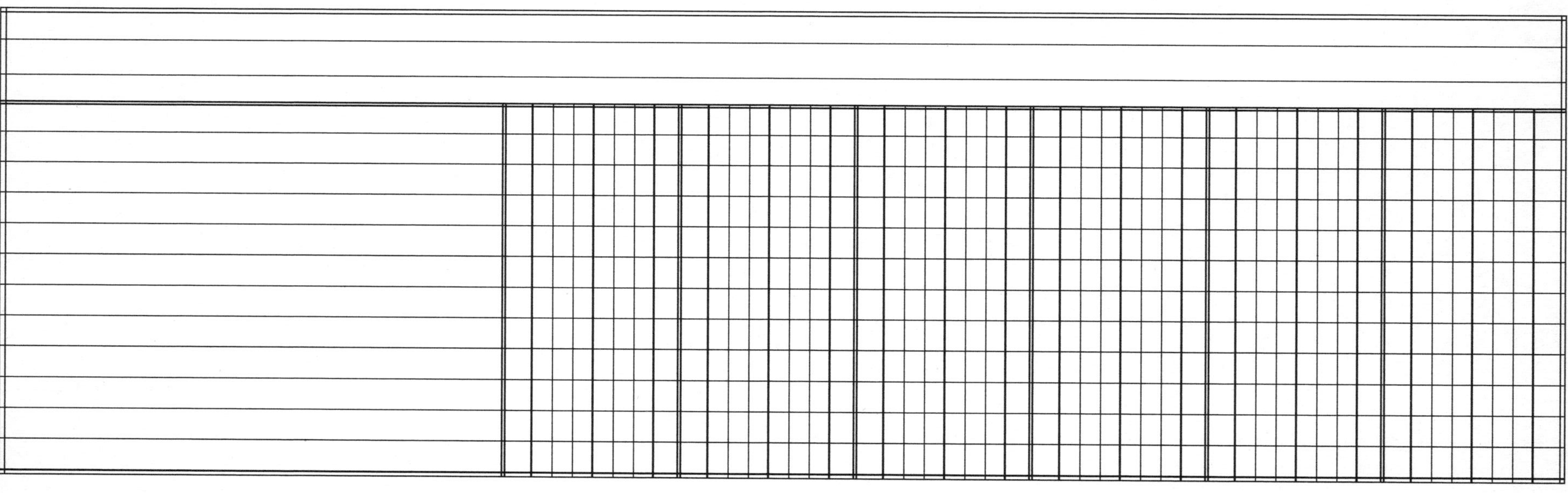

COMPUTATIONS:

NAME
SECTION
DATE

P10-4A
(Continued)

Requirement 1 (Continued)

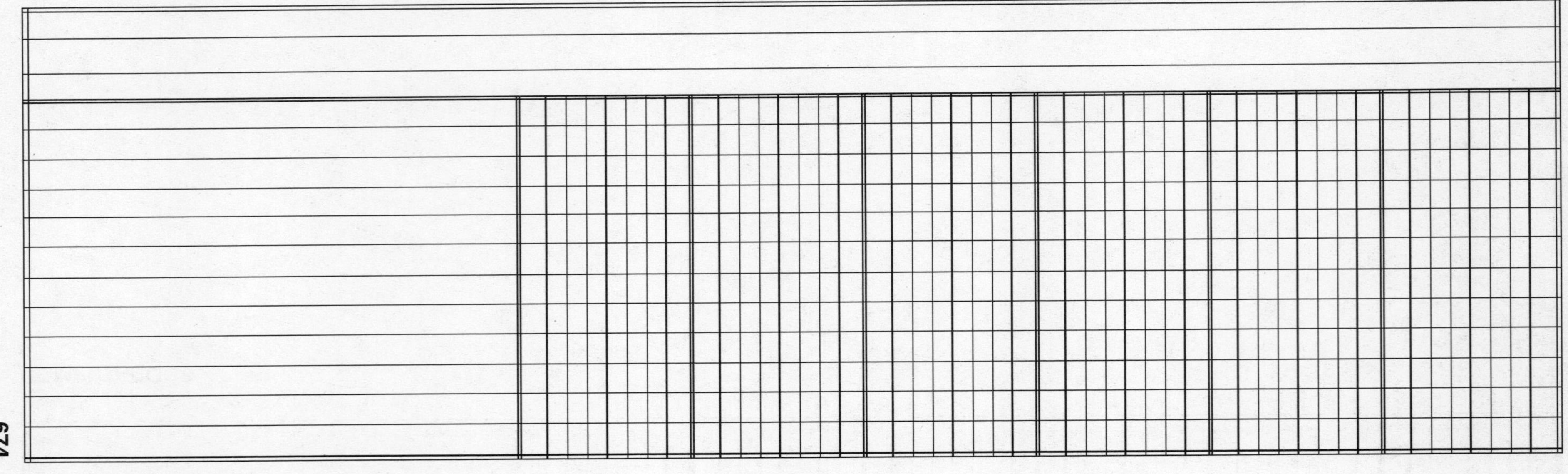

COMPUTATIONS:

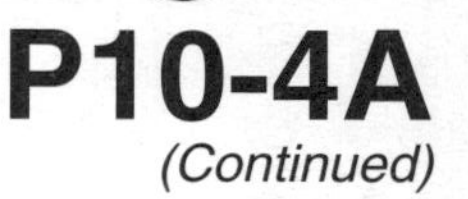

NAME
SECTION
DATE

P10-4A
(Continued)

Requirement 1 (Continued)

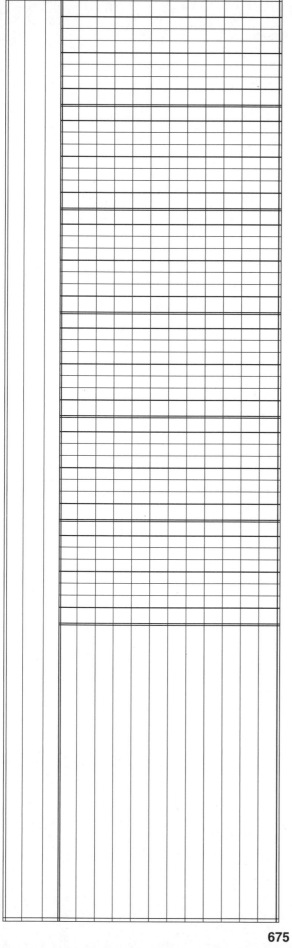

COMPUTATIONS:

NAME
SECTION
DATE

Requirement 2

P10-4A
(Continued)

NAME
SECTION
DATE

P10-5A

General Journal

DATE		ACCOUNT TITLES AND EXPLANATION	POST REF.	DEBIT	CREDIT

COMPUTATIONS:

NAME
SECTION
DATE

P10-5A
(Continued)

General Journal

DATE	ACCOUNT TITLES AND EXPLANATION	POST REF.	DEBIT	CREDIT

COMPUTATIONS:

NAME
SECTION
DATE

P10-6A

Requirements 1 – 3

NAME
SECTION
DATE

P10-7A

Part 1

General Journal

DATE		ACCOUNT TITLES AND EXPLANATION	POST REF.	DEBIT	CREDIT

NAME
SECTION
DATE

P10-7A
(Continued)

Part 2

Requirement 1

General Journal				
DATE	ACCOUNT TITLES AND EXPLANATION	POST REF.	DEBIT	CREDIT

Requirement 2

Part 3

General Journal				
DATE	ACCOUNT TITLES AND EXPLANATION	POST REF.	DEBIT	CREDIT

NAME
SECTION
DATE

P10-8A

Requirement 1

General Journal				
DATE	ACCOUNT TITLES AND EXPLANATION	POST REF.	DEBIT	CREDIT

NAME
SECTION
DATE

Requirement 1 (Continued)

P10-8A
(Continued)

General Journal

DATE		ACCOUNT TITLES AND EXPLANATION	POST REF.	DEBIT	CREDIT

NAME
SECTION
DATE

Requirement 2

P10-8A
(Continued)

NAME
SECTION
DATE

P10-9A

Requirements 1 & 2

General Journal				
DATE	ACCOUNT TITLES AND EXPLANATION	POST REF.	DEBIT	CREDIT

NAME
SECTION
DATE

Requirement 3

P10-9A
(Continued)

NAME
SECTION
DATE

P10-1B

Requirement 1

ITEM	LAND	LAND IMPROVEMENTS	OFFICE BUILDING	MAINTENANCE SHED	FURNITURE

COMPUTATIONS:

NAME
SECTION
DATE

Requirement 2

P10-1B
(Continued)

General Journal

DATE		ACCOUNT TITLES AND EXPLANATION	POST REF.	DEBIT	CREDIT

COMPUTATIONS:

NAME
SECTION
DATE

P10-2B

General Journal

DATE		ACCOUNT TITLES AND EXPLANATION	POST REF.	DEBIT	CREDIT

NAME
SECTION
DATE

P10-2B
(Continued)

General Journal

DATE		ACCOUNT TITLES AND EXPLANATION	POST REF.	DEBIT	CREDIT

NAME
SECTION
DATE

P10-3B

NAME
SECTION
DATE

P10-4B

Requirement 1

COMPUTATIONS:

NAME
SECTION
DATE

P10-4B
(Continued)

Requirement 1 (Continued)

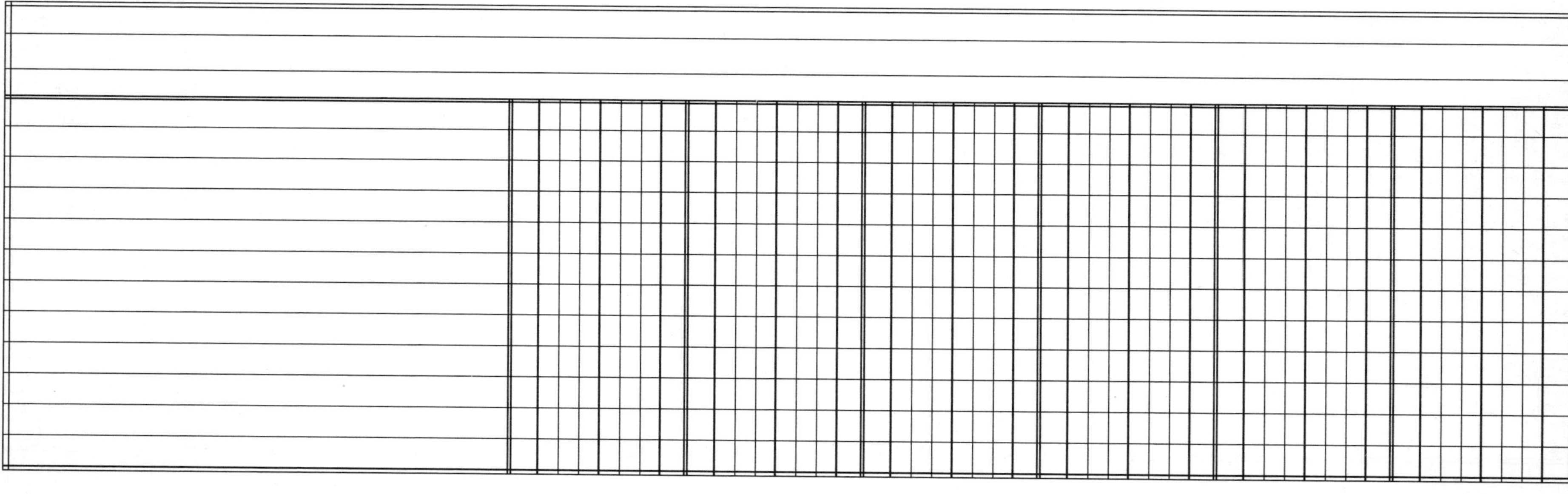

COMPUTATIONS:

P10-4B
(Continued)

NAME
SECTION
DATE

Requirement 1 (Continued)

COMPUTATIONS:

NAME
SECTION
DATE

Requirement 2

P10-4B
(Continued)

NAME
SECTION
DATE

P10-5B

General Journal

DATE	ACCOUNT TITLES AND EXPLANATION	POST REF.	DEBIT	CREDIT

COMPUTATIONS:

NAME
SECTION
DATE

P10-5B

(Continued)

General Journal

DATE		ACCOUNT TITLES AND EXPLANATION	POST REF.	DEBIT	CREDIT

COMPUTATIONS:

NAME
SECTION
DATE

P10-6B

Requirements 1 – 3

NAME
SECTION
DATE

P10-7B

Part 1

General Journal				
DATE	ACCOUNT TITLES AND EXPLANATION	POST REF.	DEBIT	CREDIT

NAME
SECTION
DATE

Part 2

P10-7B
(Continued)

Requirement 1

General Journal				
DATE	ACCOUNT TITLES AND EXPLANATION	POST REF.	DEBIT	CREDIT

Requirement 2

Part 3

General Journal				
DATE	ACCOUNT TITLES AND EXPLANATION	POST REF.	DEBIT	CREDIT

NAME
SECTION
DATE

P10-8B

Requirement 1

General Journal

DATE		ACCOUNT TITLES AND EXPLANATION	POST REF.	DEBIT	CREDIT

NAME
SECTION
DATE

Requirement 1 (Continued)

P10-8B
(Continued)

General Journal

DATE	ACCOUNT TITLES AND EXPLANATION	POST REF.	DEBIT	CREDIT

NAME
SECTION
DATE

P10-8B
(Continued)

Requirement 2

NAME
SECTION
DATE

P10-9B

Requirements 1 & 2

General Journal

DATE		ACCOUNT TITLES AND EXPLANATION	POST REF.	DEBIT	CREDIT

NAME
SECTION
DATE

Requirement 3

P10-9B
(Continued)

NAME
SECTION
DATE

P10-1C

Question 1

NAME
SECTION
DATE

Question 2

P10-1C
(Continued)

NAME
SECTION
DATE

P10-2C

COMPUTATIONS:

NAME
SECTION
DATE

Decision Problem

Requirement 1

ACCOUNT TITLE	KRUG ASSOCIATES	TSUI CO.

COMPUTATIONS:

NAME
SECTION
DATE

Decision Problem

(Continued)

Requirement 2

NAME
SECTION
DATE

Financial Statement Problem

Requirements 1 – 5

NAME
SECTION
DATE

Financial Statement Problem

(Continued)

Requirements 1 – 5 (Continued)

NAME
SECTION
DATE

Chapter 11

E11-1

General Journal				
DATE	ACCOUNT TITLES AND EXPLANATION	POST REF.	DEBIT	CREDIT

NAME
SECTION
DATE

E11-2

General Journal

DATE	ACCOUNT TITLES AND EXPLANATION	POST REF.	DEBIT	CREDIT

NAME
SECTION
DATE

E11-3

	2004	2005	2006	2007

COMPUTATIONS:

NAME
SECTION
DATE

E11-4

NAME
SECTION
DATE

E11-5

NAME
SECTION
DATE

E11-6

Requirement 1

General Journal

DATE		ACCOUNT TITLES AND EXPLANATION	POST REF.	DEBIT	CREDIT

Requirement 2

NAME
SECTION
DATE

E11-7

Requirement 1

General Journal

DATE		ACCOUNT TITLES AND EXPLANATION	POST REF.	DEBIT	CREDIT

Requirement 2

NAME
SECTION
DATE

E11-8

Requirement 1

General Journal				
DATE	ACCOUNT TITLES AND EXPLANATION	POST REF.	DEBIT	CREDIT

Requirement 2

NAME
SECTION
DATE

E11-9

Requirement 1

General Journal

DATE		ACCOUNT TITLES AND EXPLANATION	POST REF.	DEBIT	CREDIT

Requirement 2

NAME
SECTION
DATE

E11-10

NAME
SECTION
DATE

E11-11

General Journal

DATE		ACCOUNT TITLES AND EXPLANATION	POST REF.	DEBIT	CREDIT

NAME
SECTION
DATE

E11-12

Requirements 1 and 2

NAME
SECTION
DATE

E11-13

NAME
SECTION
DATE

E11-14

Requirement 1

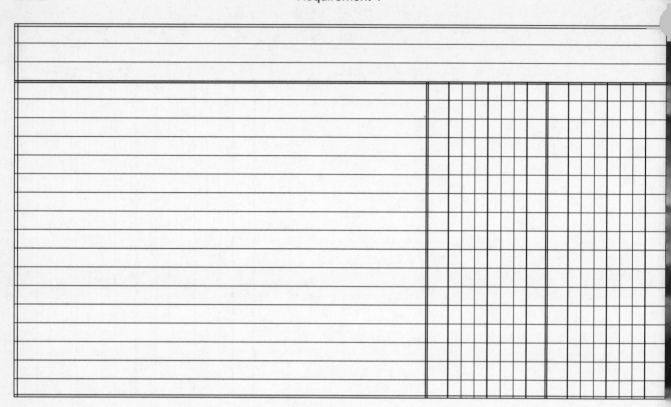

Requirement 2

General Journal

DATE		ACCOUNT TITLES AND EXPLANATION	POST REF.	DEBIT	CREDIT

NAME
SECTION
DATE

E11-15

General Journal

DATE		ACCOUNT TITLES AND EXPLANATION	POST REF.	DEBIT	CREDIT

COMPUTATIONS:

NAME
SECTION
DATE

E11-16

NAME
SECTION
DATE

E11-17

Requirements 1 & 2

COMPUTATIONS:

NAME
SECTION
DATE

E11-18

Requirements 1 & 2

NAME
SECTION
DATE

Beyond the Numbers 11-1

Requirements 1 – 3

NAME
SECTION
DATE

Beyond the Numbers 11-2

Situations a – c

NAME
SECTION
DATE

Ethical Issue

NAME
SECTION
DATE

P11-1A

General Journal

DATE	ACCOUNT TITLES AND EXPLANATION	POST REF.	DEBIT	CREDIT

NAME
SECTION
DATE

P11-1A

(Continued)

General Journal

DATE	ACCOUNT TITLES AND EXPLANATION	POST REF.	DEBIT	CREDIT

NAME
SECTION
DATE

P11-2A

NAME
SECTION
DATE

P11-3A

Requirement 1

SUPPLY MISSING PAYROLL AMOUNTS

Employee Earnings:

(a) Straight-time earnings .... ______

(b) Overtime pay .... $ 6,997

(c) Total employee earnings .... ______

Deductions and Net Pay:

(d) Withheld income tax 17,852

(e) Canada Pension Plan 3,584

(f) Employment Insurance 2,243

(g) Dental and drug insurance .... $ 778

(h) Total deductions .... ______

(i) Net pay 68,924

Accounts Debited:

(j) Salary Expense 33,234

(k) Wage Expense .... ______

(l) Sales Commission Expense 29,678

Requirement 2

General Journal

DATE		ACCOUNT TITLES AND EXPLANATION	POST REF.	DEBIT	CREDIT

NAME
SECTION
DATE

P11-4A

Requirement 1

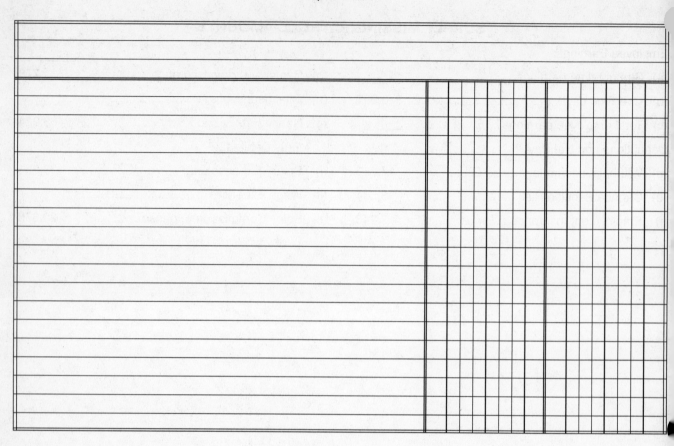

Requirement 2

NAME
SECTION
DATE

Requirement 3

P11-4A
(Continued)

General Journal

DATE		ACCOUNT TITLES AND EXPLANATION	POST REF.	DEBIT	CREDIT

NAME
SECTION
DATE

P11-5A

Requirements 1 & 2

NAME
SECTION
DATE

Requirements 1 & 2 (Continued)

P11-5A
(Continued)

NAME
SECTION
DATE

P11-5A
(Continued)

Requirement 3

Requirement 4

NAME
SECTION
DATE

P11-6A

Requirements 1 & 3

The foldout work sheet to solve this problem can be found in the back of the book.

Requirements 2 & 3

General Journal

DATE	ACCOUNT TITLES AND EXPLANATION	POST REF.	DEBIT	CREDIT

NAME
SECTION
DATE

Requirements 2 & 3

P11-6A

(Continued)

General Journal

DATE		ACCOUNT TITLES AND EXPLANATION	POST REF.	DEBIT	CREDIT

Requirement 4

NAME
SECTION
DATE

P11-7A

NAME
SECTION
DATE

P11-8A

Requirement 1

General Journal				
DATE	ACCOUNT TITLES AND EXPLANATION	POST REF.	DEBIT	CREDIT

NAME
SECTION
DATE

Requirement 1 (Continued)

P11-8A
(Continued)

General Journal

DATE		ACCOUNT TITLES AND EXPLANATION	POST REF.	DEBIT	CREDIT

NAME
SECTION
DATE

Requirement 1 (Continued)

P11-8A
(Continued)

General Journal

DATE		ACCOUNT TITLES AND EXPLANATION	POST REF.	DEBIT	CREDIT

NAME
SECTION
DATE

Requirement 1 (Continued)

P11-8A
(Continued)

General Journal

DATE		ACCOUNT TITLES AND EXPLANATION	POST REF.	DEBIT	CREDIT

NAME
SECTION
DATE

Requirement 2

P11-8A
(Continued)

NAME
SECTION
DATE

P11-9A

Requirement 1

General Journal

DATE		ACCOUNT TITLES AND EXPLANATION	POST REF.	DEBIT	CREDIT

NAME
SECTION
DATE

Requirement 1 (Continued)

P11-9A
(Continued)

General Journal

DATE		ACCOUNT TITLES AND EXPLANATION	POST REF.	DEBIT	CREDIT

NAME
SECTION
DATE

Requirement 2

P11-9A
(Continued)

NAME
SECTION
DATE

P11-1B

General Journal				
DATE	ACCOUNT TITLES AND EXPLANATION	POST REF.	DEBIT	CREDIT

NAME
SECTION
DATE

P11-1B
(Continued)

General Journal

DATE		ACCOUNT TITLES AND EXPLANATION	POST REF.	DEBIT	CREDIT

NAME
SECTION
DATE

P11-2B

NAME
SECTION
DATE

P11-3B

Requirement 1

SUPPLY MISSING PAYROLL AMOUNTS

Employee Earnings:		Deductions and Net Pay (cont.):	
(a) Straight-time earnings	$19,947	(g) Medical insurance	$ 541
(b) Overtime pay	_______	(h) Total deductions	7,147
(c) Total employee earnings	_______	(i) Net pay	18,395
Deductions and Net Pay:		**Accounts Debited:**	
(d) Withheld imcome tax	5,109	(j) Salary Expense	_______
(e) Canada Pension Plan	_______	(k) Wage Expense	6,938
(f) Employment Insurance	536	(l) Sales Commission Expense	1,681

Requirement 2

General Journal

DATE		ACCOUNT TITLES AND EXPLANATION	POST REF.	DEBIT	CREDIT

NAME
SECTION
DATE

P11-4B

Requirement 1

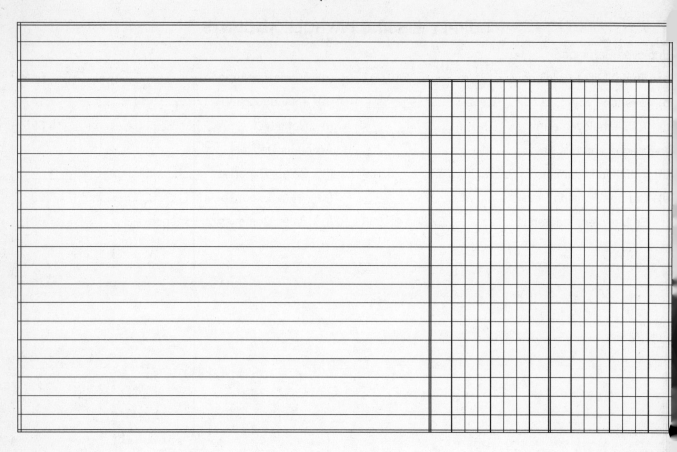

Requirement 2

NAME
SECTION
DATE

Requirement 3

P11-4B
(Continued)

General Journal

DATE		ACCOUNT TITLES AND EXPLANATION	POST REF.	DEBIT	CREDIT

NAME
SECTION
DATE

P11-5B

Requirements 1 & 2

NAME
SECTION
DATE

Requirement 3

P11-5B
(Continued)

NAME
SECTION
DATE

P11-6B

Requirements 1 & 3

The foldout work sheet to solve this problem can be found in the back of the book.

Requirements 2 & 3

General Journal

DATE	ACCOUNT TITLES AND EXPLANATION	POST REF.	DEBIT	CREDIT

NAME
SECTION
DATE

P11-6B
(Continued)

Requirements 2 – 3

General Journal				
DATE	ACCOUNT TITLES AND EXPLANATION	POST REF.	DEBIT	CREDIT

Requirement 4

NAME
SECTION
DATE

P11-7B

NAME
SECTION
DATE

P11-8B

Requirement 1

General Journal

DATE		ACCOUNT TITLES AND EXPLANATION	POST REF.	DEBIT	CREDIT

NAME
SECTION
DATE

Requirement 1 (Continued)

P11-8B
(Continued)

General Journal

DATE		ACCOUNT TITLES AND EXPLANATION	POST REF.	DEBIT	CREDIT

NAME
SECTION
DATE

Requirement 1 (Continued)

P11-8B
(Continued)

General Journal

DATE		ACCOUNT TITLES AND EXPLANATION	POST REF.	DEBIT	CREDIT

NAME
SECTION
DATE

P11-8B

Requirement 1 (Continued)

General Journal

DATE	ACCOUNT TITLES AND EXPLANATION	POST REF.	DEBIT	CREDIT

NAME
SECTION
DATE

P11-8B

(Continued)

Requirement 2

NAME
SECTION
DATE

P11-9B

Requirement 1

General Journal

DATE		ACCOUNT TITLES AND EXPLANATION	POST REF.	DEBIT	CREDIT

NAME
SECTION
DATE

P11-9B
(Continued)

Requirement 1 (Continued)

General Journal

DATE		ACCOUNT TITLES AND EXPLANATION	POST REF.	DEBIT	CREDIT

NAME
SECTION
DATE

Requirement 2

P11-9B
(Continued)

NAME
SECTION
DATE

P11-1C

NAME
SECTION
DATE

P11-2C

Requirement 1

NAME
SECTION
DATE

P11-2C
(Continued)

Requirement 2

NAME
SECTION
DATE

Decision Problem

Requirements 1 – 3

NAME
SECTION
DATE

Decision Problem

(Continued)

Requirements 1 – 3

NAME
SECTION
DATE

Financial Statement Problem

Requirement 1

General Journal

DATE		ACCOUNT TITLES AND EXPLANATION	POST REF.	DEBIT	CREDIT

NAME
SECTION
DATE

Financial Statement Problem

Requirements 2 – 4

(Continued)

NAME
SECTION
DATE

Comprehensive Problem for Part 2

Requirement 1

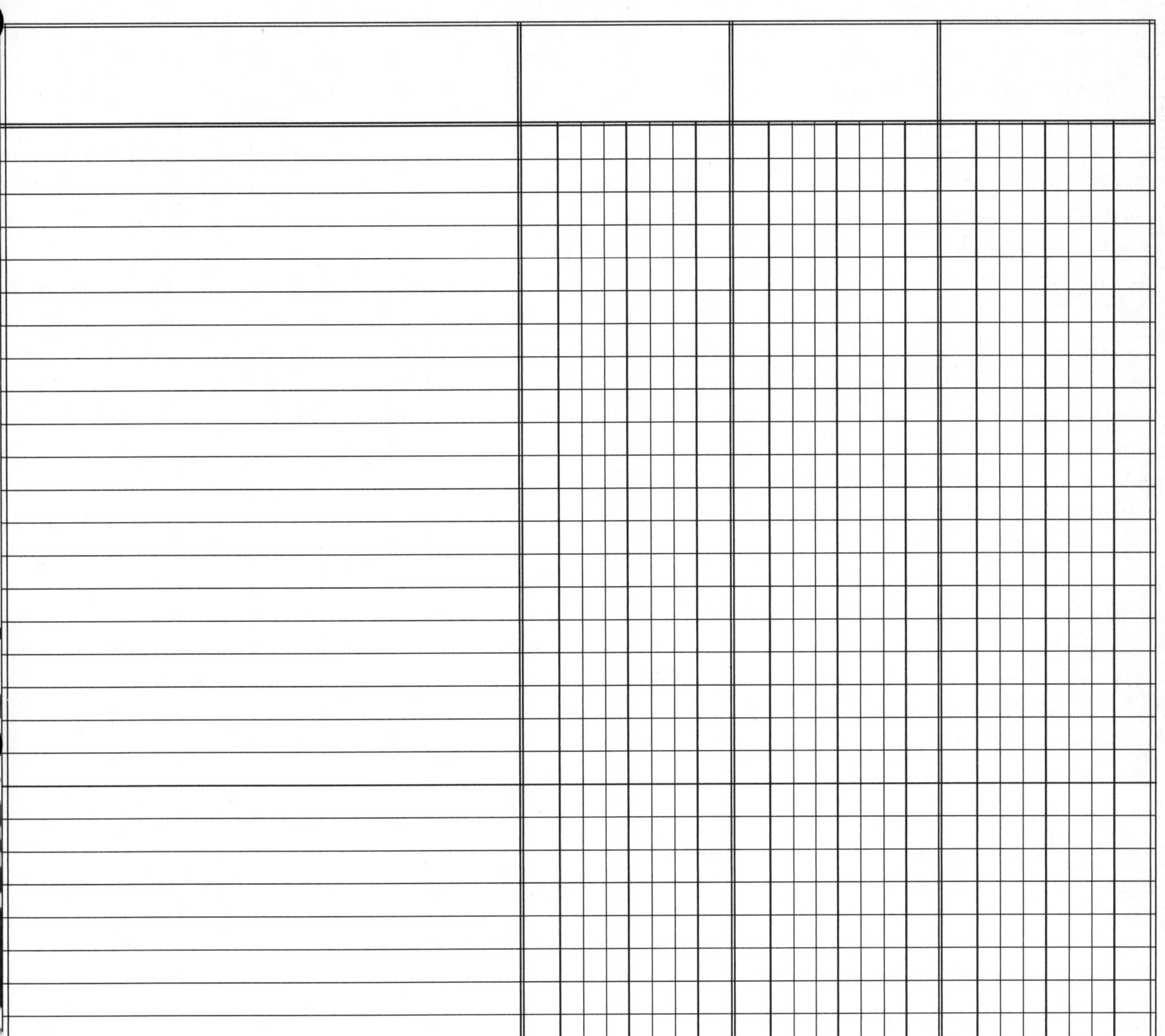

NAME
SECTION
DATE

Comprehensive Problem for Part 2

(Continued)

Requirement 2

NAME
SECTION
DATE

Comprehensive Problem for Part 2

(Continued)

Requirement 3